The Together Company

REWARDING WHAT MATTERS MOST TO
PEOPLE AND ORGANISATIONS

Raymond Robertson

Cogent

Cogent

Published by Cogent Publishing in 2007

PO Box 1426
Huddersfield
HD1 9AW
United Kingdom

A British Library Cataloguing in Publication record is available for this publication.

ISBN 978-0-9554161-0-1

Printed and bound in Great Britain by The Charlesworth Group, Wakefield, West Yorkshire.

Available from all good bookshops. In case of difficulty contact Cogent Publishing on (+44) 870 2407885.

About the author

Raymond Robertson is a leading authority on reward management and is Director of Strategic Reward, one of the UK's leading specialist reward consulting firms. Ray advises a wide range of organisations on the reward implications of business strategy and how reward can be used to increase employee engagement and business performance. His clients include Manchester United, Whitbread, ABB, Porsche Cars, Greggs, Cheshire Building Society and Guardian Newspapers.

Ray speaks about reward at a variety of events around the UK, including seminars, employers' forums, business clubs and in-company events.

He is a regular contributor to Stakeholder Satisfaction, a magazine about creating value for customers, employees and shareholders. His published articles include "Rewarding contribution", "Creating a recognition culture", "Fast guide to attraction and retention" and "Balanced scorecard: putting it into practice".

Ray has a B.Sc. (Production Engineering) from Nottingham Trent University and a postgraduate DMS from Glasgow University. Ray is a Chartered Fellow of the Chartered Institute of Personnel and Development.

Author's contact details:
team@strategicreward.com
telephone 01454 618995

To my mother and father, both now sadly gone. They definitely believed in togetherness.

Acknowledgements

This book has been a journey, a journey which would not have been possible without the support and encouragement of colleagues and friends. I would like to thank, in particular, Nigel Hill from The Leadership Factor, for his wise counsel, guidance and detailed comments at various stages of the book.

I am also extremely grateful to Roberto Ponte from Infineum International, Seth Russell from BBC Worldwide, Alison McMullen from Animal (sports retailer) and Janet Hill from The Leadership Factor who provided detailed comments and insights to the earlier draft of the book.

Many companies have kindly contributed material for the case studies in the book. I would like to acknowledge Trevor Blackman from The Royal Bank of Scotland Group, Sharon Quinn and Jo Rackham from Whitbread, Julie Gregory from BAA, Philip Addison from Accor UK, Janet Oldham from Miller Insurance Services, Anthony Lawler from Manchester United, Debbie Thomson from Starbucks Coffee Company, Andrew Walker from Scottish Water, Joanne Kelly from ABB Engineering Services and Ruth Hutchison from T.G.I. Friday's. I am grateful to them for allowing their stories to be told.

A final heartfelt thanks to my wife Louise who has been an enormous support and given encouragement throughout my writing.

Contents

Detailed Contents

PART TWO

CHAPTER EIGHT
REWARDING TEAM EXCELLENCE

CHAPTER NINE
REWARDING CUSTOMER SATISFACTION

PART THREE

CHAPTER TWELVE
CUSTOMISED REWARD STRATEGIES

CHAPTER THIRTEEN
RECOGNITION AND CELEBRATION

CHAPTER SIXTEEN
THE FIVE BUSINESS REASONS TO BECOME A TOGETHER COMPANY   213

Preface

The world of work has changed forever. The balance of power has shifted irreversibly from the organisation to the employee.

Employees today are clear about what they want from organisations and what they are prepared to give in return. Their loyalty often lies more with their CV than it does with the company they work for, so they think nothing of changing jobs six times before they are thirty years of age. Many, especially knowledge workers, are highly mobile. An increasing number of them work from home, for at least part of the working week – and even that's changed. A wide range of flexible working options now exist alongside the traditional 9 to 5 day.

Employees' concept of fairness has changed too, from "equal" to "worth". Train drivers can earn £40,000 a year. Secretaries may have shares worth thousands of pounds in their company. A £1m bonus in the City of London no longer makes the headlines. Employees can hand pick their own individual mix of reward options to best suit their needs and lifestyle.

To compete in this world, business leaders need to know how to engage talented people and ensure their commitment to business goals. And because rewards, financial and non financial, are a powerful communicator of a company's values, direction and business priorities they have a crucial role in business success. To compete in this world, you have to become a Together Company.

In my thirty years in HR, I haven't seen many Together Companies. I've seen plenty of organisations where employees don't understand business objectives, work in silos and don't know how their rewards are determined. Perhaps this is because being a Together Company isn't easy; but it's possible, as demonstrated by the case studies in this book. If this book gives you just a handful of good ideas to make your organisation a Together Company, I'll have exceeded my objectives.

CHAPTER ONE
The Together Company

Imagine a company where people work together toward common objectives which they all understand and agree with; where a clear set of values guide everybody in behaving in ways which are right for customers and long term growth of the organisation; and where people feel valued for the contribution they make. This company believes passionately that people are its greatest asset – without people, the business will not succeed. This ethos is summed up in the words of John Spedan Lewis, Founder, The John Lewis Partnership[1]:

"The Partnership was meant to enable people to feel that they might be making a contribution of real value to the ceaseless experimenting that is necessary to human progress. It was meant for people who need not only something to live by but something to live for."

This is the very essence of The Together Company.

Communicating what matters most

But The Together Company knows that just because its business plan sets out common objectives and values, it doesn't mean employees know what these are, so it goes to considerable lengths to ensure that they do. Philip Addison, Human Resources Director, Accor UK & Ireland Hotels, puts it this way:

"Business Leaders often take some of the basics for granted and assume that employees know what's important if the business is to succeed, what's expected of them and what they can receive in return. But, if we, the Business Leaders, don't set out clearly what's expected of employees and what we'll provide in return, how can we possibly expect employees to know what's important to our business? Developing our vision and values with them really helped us clarify our own thinking".

Achieving common objectives and realising long term vision are, of course, rarely in the hands of one person or a small group of people. When members of David Lloyd Leisure for example, visit their Club for a work-out, a swim and a (healthy) meal afterwards, their "member experience" is determined by the behaviour of the employees they meet during their visit. That's why organisations like David Lloyd Leisure keep employees informed about how well the business is performing in relation to what matters most to its success – and reward them accordingly.

This is the way of The Together Company. Its business leaders, managers and employees engage in regular dialogue about what matters most to the organisation and to employees. Figure 1.1 shows how Starbucks Coffee Company discusses and communicates what matters most. Everybody in The Together Company is honest about the way they see things – financial results, customer satisfaction, productivity, teamwork, good news or bad news. By being honest, people help to create a culture where continuous improvement is the order of the day and, when things don't go according to plan, everybody is keen to get performance back on track as quickly as possible. This "learn from the past – focus on the future" attitude is in stark contrast to the blame culture of many organisations, especially when results fall short of expectations. Business leaders in The Together Company are honest too about what it can afford – in relation to pay reviews, training programmes, new facilities and much more, and why.

Working together

This "working smarter / working together" attitude means employees in The Together Company want to do their best and get better, so performance feedback and coaching at all times, not just "difficult" times, encourages them to develop and improve. Companies like BAA recognise this by measuring "how results are achieved" not just "what is achieved" and rewards reflect achievements in relation to the whats and the hows.

The journey to The Together Company requires people, at all levels, to work together not against each other. Teamwork and co-operation between people, within teams and between teams, is highly-prized. That doesn't mean there isn't room for individual flair and initiative: of course there is, providing the focus is team or organisational objectives rather than, for example, a personal objective to raise the individual's profile among business leaders when this is completely inappropriate.

Malingerers on the other hand – people who do as little as they can get away with (we all know who they are) or who go out of their way to behave in ways that destroy

---

FIGURE 1.1   Starbucks Coffee Company:
Discussing and communicating what matters most

Starbucks Coffee Company (employees are called partners) allows partners the opportunity to get involved in the business through "Partner Blend". This gives a voice to partners' views through a dedicated group of elected representatives across all of Starbucks who meet two to four times a year with members of the UK leadership team.

Gordon Lyle, Vice-President, Human Resources, EMEA says[2]:

"Starbucks has a vision of building an extraordinary company….together. You simply could not find a better way than Partner Blend to allow partner reps and members of the UK and Ireland Leadership Team to directly and openly discuss and challenge the decisions that will allow Starbucks to move onwards and upwards in the UK".

Lots of issues are raised through Partner Blend, such as HR, marketing, store development and supply chain operations. A selection of the issues raised in Partner Blend's first year and the company's response are given below:

"You've said you want other innovations to help reduce wastage."

Our commitment is to give stores an electronic ordering system that will make forward re-forecasting much easier and will allow stores to change their orders more easily.

"You've said you want information about access improvements for customers."

We have identified alterations that need to be made to our stores to improve access for all our customers. Over the next two years these changes will be made in a staged process. Some of the initial changes will include doorbells for customers who need assistance entering the store, better signage within the store and temporary ramps for disabled customers.

"You've said you want encouragement to get involved in Corporate Social Responsibility."

We have committed to this through a number of partner incentives including funding for up to two paid days per year to work on a partner's chosen cause, a partner from each region receiving two weeks paid time off to work with a charity, and the fantastic "Life's Dream" competition.

---

customer value and upset working relationships – have no place in The Together Company. And business leaders will be ruthless about this. As Collins and Porras point out in "Built To Last"[3] the bad fit employees are "ejected like a virus". Cliques and factions who blame each other when things go wrong are simply not tolerated;

neither are people who openly express negative views about the company's motives, ethics or performance.

Just like The John Lewis Partnership does, The Together Company creates a "sense of ownership" among employees, so that they "think like owners" and genuinely feel that their personal success and the company's are tied together. When the company succeeds, employees share in that success. This is a meritocracy at work, not a false hierarchy that alienates employees from each other by favouring the few, financially, at the expense of the majority. Howard Schultz, Chairman, Starbucks Coffee Company, expresses this powerfully in his book "Pour Your Heart Into It"[4] when he says:

"There is no more precious commodity than the relationship of trust and confidence a company has with its employees. If people believe management is not fairly sharing the rewards, they will feel alienated. Once they start distrusting management, the company's future is compromised".

This is why business leaders in The Together Company work tirelessly to build and retain trust and confidence by behaving and acting in exemplar ways. They are the role model for "the way we do things around here". But it takes more than business leaders who are exemplars to build The Together Company. It involves creating a truly great place to work which attracts and retains the best talent and where people feel they do rewarding work. And that's a lot to do with intangible factors or "soft rewards" such as job challenge and interest, freedom and autonomy, employees' needs at different stages of their life and reputation of the organisation.

These aspects are reflected in The Royal Bank of Scotland Group's employee proposition which is designed to attract, engage and retain the best talent. The proposition comprises eight areas[5]: total reward, work itself, recognition, performance and development, relationships, leadership, product brands and reputation, work-life balance and physical environment.

The Together Company, in a nutshell, is about shared vision and values, people working together to satisfy customers and generate profits for long term growth, and business leaders who inspire employees to excel at everything they do.

And there's one more, crucially important characteristic – the organisation has a successful reward policy. It's successful because it engages employees in the work that they do, and that leads to improved business results. So, what's the secret of its success? One simple, but very fundamental reason: it recognises the specific business needs of the organisation and the personal needs of the people who work in it. People in The Together Company really feel that rewards match their contribution and that they have been determined in a fair and consistent way.

Put all this together and you have an outstanding organisation, one that business leaders would like to create; an organisation we would choose to work for; an organisation with a highly successful business record and a great future for everybody who works there and is associated with it – employees, customers and shareholders.

Welcome to The Together Company – rewarding what matters most to people and organisations.

Rewarding what matters most
The three-part reward framework in The Together Company

Rewards are a powerful communicator of business direction and values, so they matter a lot in terms of togetherness. But, too often, organisations don't actually reward what they say they value, so they end up rewarding things that don't contribute to business success and that sends mixed messages about what matters most. It's also a complete waste of money. Classic examples of such "disconnects or misalignment" I come across frequently are:

- Paying more to people just because they've been there longest
- Rewarding individual performance only when the company wants teamwork
- No incentive for people to learn and apply new skills that add value to the business
- No reward for effective business leadership, and
- Lack of recognition for innovation.

Reward isn't just about pay, of course, although lots of organisations are obsessed with it! In my opinion, they over-estimate the role of pay and under-estimate the role of non-financial rewards in engaging people in their work. Employees want rewarding work – to have a workplace which inspires them to give their best and to enjoy their time at work. This is why reward in The Together Company is set in the context of everything employees value in the employment relationship – financial reward, non-financial recognition, personal learning and development opportunities and a supportive and enabling work environment. These aspects are grouped together under a "Total Reward" brand by an increasing number of organisations today.

Fortunately, the number of HR executives and senior managers who believe there's an off-the-shelf set of reward practices which can satisfy business requirements and people's needs in any organisation, whatever its size, complexity and business context is dwindling rapidly. This point was brought home to me recently when I met, for the first time, the Chairman of a company which is now one of my clients. He asked me "In all your experience, what's the best way to reward people – there must be some ideal practices?" I replied: "There's no such thing as an ideal reward practice, no panacea, although lots of people are looking for one. But successful reward practices do exist and that's because they focus on people behaving in ways that are right for customers and financial success. These practices take into account also the things that really matter to employees, such as fair performance review, rewards that match their contribution and thanks for doing a great job". The Chairman continued: "I'm glad you said that: I agree. I think we can do business together. If you'd said differently, this meeting would be ending very shortly!"

Reward is one of the largest investments The Together Company makes. Getting the optimal return on that investment means reward must focus on two, mutually dependent, demands:

- **Results that matter most to the organisation**
- **Results that matters most to the people who work in it.**

Every reward practice and reward process has to satisfy these two demands. Not surprisingly, there are lots of ways in which this can be achieved. These are the substance of this book. But because individual reward practices, just like employees, need to work together, there's a set of principles – I call them "the six reward values" – which guide reward design and implementation in The Together Company. These are shown in the box below.

> **The six reward values of The Together Company**
>
> 1. **Business-aligned**
> 2. **Rewarding excellence**
> 3. **Sharing in success**
> 4. **Choice and flexibility**
> 5. **Fairness**
> 6. **Rewarding work**

Business-aligned almost speaks for itself. It's about aligning reward, business priorities and the values that guide people in their day-to-day work. Excellence is central to everything The Together Company does, so rewarding it makes good business sense. This is a far cry from the "entitlement" culture of many organisations in which mediocrity is the norm. If people help create business success, they should share in it – financially and non-financially.

Today's workforce is more diverse than ever before, so a one-size-fits all approach to reward no longer matches reality and offering choice and flexibility over rewards that suit people best (at different life stages) is good use of money. Even if reward design is "technically sound" (which it always should be, of course) its impact on employee engagement and business results will be limited unless employees feel it's fair in relation to what they do.

Some reward practices, like fashion, come and go. Others stand the test of time. And there are some aspects of reward that you always have to get right. For these reasons, reward in The Together Company operates within a flexible three-part framework which adapts to the changing needs of the business and the people work who work in it. The key elements of the framework are set out below:

Reward Essentials

These are the things The Together Company makes sure it gets right before anything else because they underpin how the people who work there are rewarded and managed more generally. In fact, it excels at them. Getting them wrong means unfairness, dissatisfaction, unsustainable costs and chaos – a recipe for business failure. That's why I call them "Reward Essentials". They're based on what I've observed works best in successful organisations – successful in terms of employee engagement which leads to improved business results. There are six Reward Essentials:

- **Rewarding performance**
- **Performance management**
- **Fair performance review**
- **A pay framework**
- **Understanding your employment market – pay and benefits**
- **Equal pay.**

Getting Reward Essentials right – building employees trust and being fair – is more important than rushing to introduce fancy reward schemes which somebody, somewhere, "thinks" are a good idea.

Reward Choices

These are the specific reward practices which support (sometimes drive) the four core business objectives of The Together Company. Some of you may be surprised that there are four only. But, when a company has a myriad of reward practices, each with lots of objectives, this leads to people taking their eyes off the ball, resources being spread too thinly and confusion among employees (shareholders and customers too) because they don't know what the business priorities are. Focus on the few, success-critical objectives is what matters most. That's why I call them "Reward Choices"and they are:

- **Rewarding team excellence**
- **Rewarding customer satisfaction**
- **Sharing in financial success**
- **Rewarding business leaders.**

Together Companies combine and tailor Reward Choices in ways which match their organisational circumstances. This might reflect size (numbers of people, for example), sector challenges (maintaining a competitive edge, for example), growth rates (rapid in one part of the business and slower elsewhere) and structure (project working, customer focused teams or the organisation as whole).

Reward Extras

These are other reward practices and processes which help build and retain a culture of "togetherness", a culture in which people really feel they are The Together Company's most important investment. I call them "Reward Extras", not because they're optional (which they aren't!) but because they're the extra, special touches which make The Together Company stand out from the crowd. They're highly visible in people's day-to-day work. They acknowledge excellence, tap into what people value as individuals and keep them informed about what matters most and what they can expect to receive in return. There are four Reward Extras:

- **Customised reward strategies**
- **Recognition and celebration**
- **A rewarding workplace**
- **Reward communications.**

Reward Extras reward and recognise what's right for the organisation, rather than imitate what others do.

In this book

This book is structured around the three-part reward framework in The Together Company. Each part is divided into chapters about the reward practices that, collectively, make up Reward Essentials, Reward Choices and Reward Extras. Step-by-step processes for developing and implementing all aspects of the reward framework are included. So too are solutions to the most commonly found problems surrounding specific reward practices.

I have used case studies and many other worked examples extensively throughout the book to show how togetherness translates into reward. However, it's probably true to say that none of the companies mentioned in the book is "totally together" in its literal sense. But I believe the case studies give a practical insight into what can be achieved by focusing on what matters most to the organisation and to the people who work in it.

Examples of how the different elements of the reward framework might work in Together Companies of different sizes or organisational circumstances are given in the section called "Is it right for you?" at the end of each chapter.

In this book I show how The Together Company makes sure people are rewarded on the basis of their contribution to business success and they feel they are.

Case study

Rewarding togetherness at David Lloyd Leisure

My first case study is David Lloyd Leisure (David Lloyd) the UK and Ireland's market leader in Racquets, Health and Fitness Clubs. I've chosen David Lloyd because it's an excellent example of a Together Company and it has been a very successful business.

David Lloyd's mission is "Inspire for life". Currently 67 clubs provide facilities that include indoor and outdoor tennis courts, indoor and outdoor swimming pools, state-of-the-art gymnasiums, group fitness sessions, beauty salons, café and restaurants and crèche facilities. David Lloyd is a subsidiary of Whitbread Group plc (Whitbread) and has over 350,000 members. It employs 5,200 people.

Achieving David Lloyd's mission is about delivering results to three groups of stakeholders: people, members and investors – and in that order. In the words of Louise Smalley, HR Director of David Lloyd:

"By taking care of our people, our members will have a great experience and want to

come back; we will deliver strong financial results for our investors and sustainable growth and new clubs for the business."

So, how does David Lloyd take care of its people, inspire them to deliver a great experience for club members and reward them for doing so, and what's been the business outcome?

Understanding what matters most to club members and inspiring people to deliver it

David Lloyd, along with all other Whitbread brands, has adopted a common approach to defining and measuring the things that lead to business success. The approach is called "WINcard" (Whitbread In Numbers) and it's based on balanced scorecard principles.

> ### Balanced Scorecard
>
> The Balanced Scorecard[6] provides a framework to translate business strategy and vision into tangible objectives and measures by which managers can navigate to success. It brings together financial, customer, internal business process and people under one performance management system. It enables managers to understand the linkages between these areas and helps them focus their efforts.

At David Lloyd, WINcard and the Club Annual Operating Plans together communicate to everybody what's expected of them. David Lloyd's Club WINcard (Figure 1.2) is prominently displayed in every club and people can see at a glance progress towards performance targets for each of the three groups of stakeholders.

But success at David Lloyd isn't just about WINcard and the mission statement. People working there must "feel the difference" and that means managers creating the right environment for everybody to create a great experience for club members. So David Lloyd created "Spirit to Inspire".

FIGURE 1.2   The Club WINcard at David Lloyd Leisure

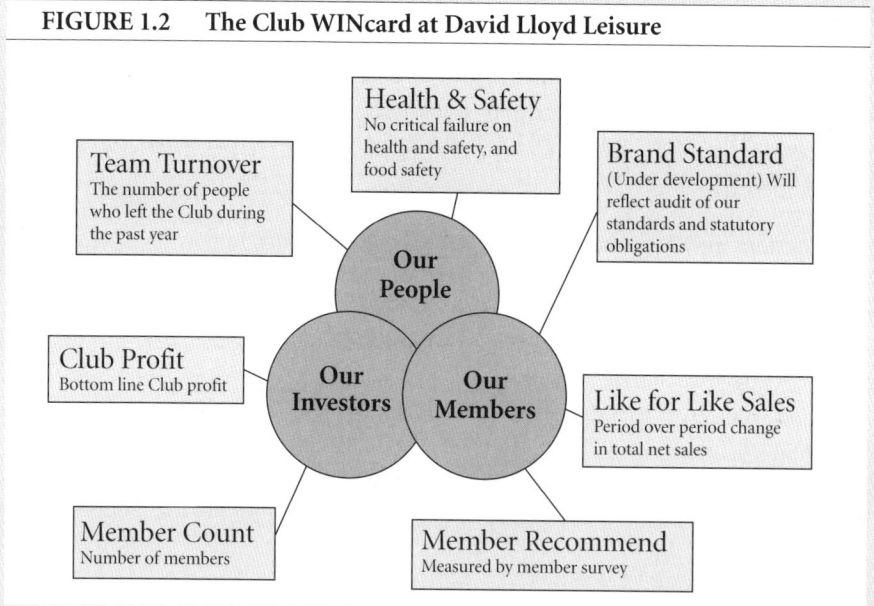

This three-day programme is attended by the management team of each club and is held at a nice location so the team can get away from daily distractions. It's run periodically for existing clubs and new ones. Spirit to Inspire was designed on the basis of research into what people were saying about working at their club, what members were saying about their experiences and the value-profit chain concept.

> ## The Value-Profit Chain
>
> **Today's employee satisfaction, loyalty and commitment strongly influences tomorrow's customer satisfaction, loyalty, and commitment and ultimately the organisation's profit and growth – a quantifiable set of associations Heskett, Sasser and Schlesinger call the value profit chain[7].**

Spirit to Inspire is run by Regional Managers who have been trained to deliver the programme, with support from HR. The programme includes presentations from David Lloyd Board members and includes training videos, quizzes, games and exercises which are designed to encourage people to work together to create great member experiences.

Before going on Spirit to Inspire, each member of the management team complete a personality type exercise and, using a standard set of questions, audit their club's performance against the Annual Operating Plan.

Day 1: Communication and teamwork. A Board member sets the context within Whitbread and managers share their personality profile and perceptions about different aspects of work at David Lloyd and how this affects their behaviour towards colleagues and club members.

Day 2: Leaders and brands. Managers say what they think makes great leaders by looking at their own experiences in, for example, work or sport. They also give their perceptions of well-known brands such as easyJet, BMW or McDonald's, even though they may not have experienced them. They use their perceptions and experiences and the 3-circle service model – basic, expected, inspirational – to build a picture of what great member experiences look like at David Lloyd.

Day 3: Service delivery. Managers look at how meeting expectations isn't enough, why club members don't come back, what brilliant service looks like and engaging their team in delivering it.

One week later, the management team goes on a one-day follow up where they present their action plan for delivering Spirit to Inspire to everyone back at their club, within 90 days. They are given facilitation skills for cascading the programme in their club but they decide how to cascade. This flexibility has been a major factor in engaging employees at club level, in the core messages from Spirit to Inspire and making it relevant to their day-to-day work.

Developing people to their full potential

But Spirit to Inspire, alone, can't guarantee that great member experiences will be delivered. That requires a pool of talented people and is why there's such a strong commitment at David Lloyd (in fact, throughout Whitbread) to developing people to their full potential. The performance review process plays the key role here. "Honest conservations" are the basis of the process and the outcomes feed into annual pay review, bonus and succession planning. David Lloyd guarantees that everybody will have a review twice a year and this commitment is measured though "Views" an employee survey carried out every six months.

Managers

Managers performance reviews take place in March and September, when their performance is assessed against the seven WINcard measures – club profit, member count, team turnover, health and safety, brand standard, like for like sales and member recommend. Performance is rated on a five point scale defined as Outstanding, Exceeding, Achieving, Growing and Unacceptable. There's an expected distribution of performance ratings but this isn't forced.

The reviews also include a career / potential assessment. Potential is rated on a ten point scale which defines the readiness for promotion and / or development and takes account of a manager's judgment, influence and drive. The potential rating is shared with the manager and possible development actions are discussed with him / her.

A key outcome from the performance review is a personal development plan which is based on the four principles of The Whitbread Way – People and Teamwork, Caring for Guests, Passion for Winning and Continuous Improvement – that underpin all David Lloyd (and Whitbread) does. The plan focuses on building strengths and priority development needs.

Team Members

For all other people, such as Lifeguards, Membership Advisors, Head Chefs, Hospitality Staff and Health and Fitness Coaches (collectively called Team Members) who work in clubs, performance review is a simplified version of the process for managers. The main performance review takes place once a year, when the focus is the team member's achievements last year and agreed actions for the coming year. In preparation for the review meeting with their manager, team members complete a form that includes two sections called:

- "How was it for you?" which covers aspects of work giving the most satisfaction, areas to build on, what might help do the job more effectively and things to improve
- "My Self Assessment" which covers the most important aspects of the team member's work – based on The Whitbread Way. The areas are:

People and Teamwork	**Appearance at work**
Caring for Members	**Punctuality on shift/meetings/appointments**
Passion for Winning	**Job knowledge**
Continuous Improvement	**Reliability**

Managers decide an overall performance rating for each team member they review, using the same five-point scale in their own reviews. Again, there's an expected distribution of performance ratings but this isn't forced. Managers also consider if the team member is ready for promotion to their next role, within their current department or in another department. This is an important aspect of succession planning at David Lloyd.

Agreed actions for the coming year are based on the Club WINcard, The Whitbread Way and Club Annual Operating Plan and follow the SMART principle: specific, measurable, agreed, realistic and time based. The completed performance review – rating, career development plan, manager's comments and employee's comments – is agreed between the manager and team member. The performance rating is very important as it gives an overall summary of performance and it's used for pay review.

Six months later, all team members have a "job chat" with their manager. This provides an opportunity to touch base about how things are going, identify if there are any challenges or opportunities and basically make sure everything is going well.

Rewarding performance / sharing in success

David Lloyd's reward strategy has a strong performance focus. It delivers this in three ways:

- **Through pay review** – which takes place annually for everyone (we look at pay review for team members)
- **Through bonus** – this applies to managers only and is linked to WINcard
- **Through "Team Workout"** – rewards for what team members do to deliver great member experiences.

Pay review for Team Members

Each job has a pay scale which has three defined points – base, middle and top. These are benchmarked against relevant organisations inside and outside the hospitality and health and fitness industries. But because market pay varies by geographic location in the UK, David Lloyd has created pay zones – there are three in the UK. Each club is allocated to a pay zone on the basis of recruitment difficulties in the Club's location. However, if a club is experiencing considerable difficulty recruiting the right person for a specific job, there is flexibility to use a pay scale from a higher paying zone.

Pay review is based on two things – performance rating and where the team member is paid in the pay scale for their job. For example, a team member rated Outstanding and paid below the middle will receive a higher increase than someone rated Growing and paid above the middle.

Bonus opportunity for managers

Managers at David Lloyd have the opportunity to earn a bonus based on performance in relation to their Club's WINcard targets. Performance is measured by "traffic lights" which works as follows:

- Green = target or better
- Amber = better than last year but below target
- Red = below last year and below target

Bonus potential varies between the three management levels: a General Manager can earn up to 100% of their salary and Heads of Department / Club Support Managers can all earn up to 25% of salary. Bonus has three different elements as outlined below:

- Bonus for "Going Green" on five WINcard measures – Like for Like Sales, Team Turnover, Member Count, Member Recommend and Health and Safety (Brand Standard is not bonusable)
- The Stakeholder Stretch: When a Club has reached 96% of club budgeted profit (for Club Support it's when the Company hits 96% of budgeted Economic Profit) an additional bonus is paid
- The Pence-in-the-Pound Driver: This applies to General Managers and Heads of Department only. If the budgeted club profit exceeds 106%, for every pound earned over 106%, the manager will earn additional bonus.

Team rewards for delivering great member experiences

The number of members at any one time is one of the easiest guides to the health and success of a David Lloyd Club. Members might well be impressed by the great facilities, but it's the people and their service skills that make the real difference. Those members enjoying their visits and appreciating great service are the ones that will recommend the club to their friends and colleagues. So, David Lloyd has a reward scheme called "Team Workout", which is about what team members will do to help their club deliver a great experience to members.

At their performance review, team members look at the priorities for their Club and team and agree with their manager what they will do in the coming 6-12 months to help meet WINcard targets. If, for example "get the basics right – service to members" is the priority, team members on reception might aim for a score of 85% on mystery member standards by treating every member like a VIP. Other team members might decide "when a member is within 5 metres of me I will greet them every time", or "every time I speak to a child member I will make eye contact at their level".

Success is rewarded for hitting the club's quarterly target on the number of members. If all quarters targets for the year are met, the rewards are £150 per year in "Leisure Vouchers" for full time team members. Payouts start at £25 per quarter for hitting the first and second quarters and rise to £50 per quarter if three or four quarters have been hit. Payments for part-time team members are pro-rated. Team members can track progress by looking at the Club WINcard, which shows the quarterly target and results month-by-month.

Tailoring benefits to match people's lifestyles

The complexity of Whitbread's business structure hasn't made a single flexible benefits plan which covers the different businesses (including David Lloyd) practical, but the creation of a central service structure recently and plans to rationalise terms and conditions across the brands may put flexible benefits on the reward agenda in the near future.

Everybody at David Lloyd takes part in the Whitbread benefits programme which has always recognised that employees want choice and flexibility, so wherever possible this has been provided within a prescribed set of benefits. The programme comprises two parts:

- Whitbread Privilege Card which offers a range of discounts throughout Whitbread. The card is given to all employees and, in addition to the discounts, gives employees an opportunity to try the "guest experience" in each of the brands for themselves
- Additional benefits which Whitbread have negotiated with other leading organisations. This is where employees are able to choose – some benefits are open to all employees and others are job related. The benefits are summarised in Figure 1.3.

FIGURE 1.3
Whitbread - Additional Benefits

Your Money
- Whitbread Sharesave
- Pensions
- Car Purchase
- Car Hire & Breakdown Cover
- Insurance – Travel & Home
- Whitbread Leisure Vouchers
- Conveyancing

Your Well-Being
- Employee Assistance Programme
- Health Plans
- Private Healthcare
- Dental Healthcare

Your Lifestyle
- Gift Ideas
- Holidays – UK & Abroad
- Days Out
- Home Learning
- Driving Lessons

Whitbread chose the route of sourcing benefits providers themselves instead of taking a 3rd party 'off the shelf' option and very strongly believe in their strategy, as Jo Rackham, the Reward Manager responsible for benefits planning at Whitbread, explains:

"We have individually tailored all benefits on offer to coincide with what our employees tell us they want and also what we believe is responsible for us as an employer to offer. Our aim is to provide a benefit to cover every key area of our employees' lives: their money; their well-being; and their lifestyle.

We scrutinise each provider to ensure they can give our employees the very best service and the very best offer we can negotiate. We frequently target the big brand names for reliability, economies of scale and as they compliment the good name of Whitbread.

It's a very successful scheme (employees tell us!) but the biggest on-going challenge is communication. You can have the best benefits scheme in the world, but unless you keep reminding people about it, they forget. So, we send monthly updates about the latest offers. We do this by including messages on pay-slips and on notice boards, and we run competitions with prizes given by our benefits providers".

Business outcomes

So, what's been the business impact of people working together and being rewarded for delivering a great experience to club members? The business results are impressive[8]:

- Growth in new member sales over the last five months of 19.4% and a fall in leavers of 7.2% for like-for-like clubs
- On the back of recent improved membership satisfaction, retention has increased to 72.4% at the year end compared to a fall of 1% in the previous year
- Total membership in the UK is at a record high.

The final word goes to Sharon Quinn, Head of Reward, Whitbread Group:

"Recent employee opinion surveys show that 96% of people have a clear understanding of their responsibilities. In addition, team turnover has improved by 10 percentage points, year on year, and 55% of our members make specific positive comments about our people".

Part one
Reward Essentials

These are the things The Together Company makes sure it gets right before anything else because they underpin how the people who work there are rewarded and managed more generally. In fact, it excels at them. Getting them wrong means unfairness, dissatisfaction, unsustainable costs and chaos – a recipe for business failure.

Rewarding performance

Business success depends on the organisation achieving what it sets out to do. People help create that success, and they want to be rewarded for it. The controversy arises over "how" – individually, team or organisationally. But if people aren't rewarded for performance or contribution, I believe this sends completely the wrong message about what matters most to the organisation. That's why rewarding performance matters.

Performance management

This is about getting better results from the organisation, teams and individuals by managing performance within a framework for agreeing goals and evaluating achievements. The emphasis is people having a shared understanding about "what matters most" and actions which people take to achieve the day-to-day delivery of results and improvements.

Fair performance review

Performance review doesn't come easily to many managers – and to employees for that matter – although most people like to know how well they are doing. Making judgments about performance, especially individual or team-based, can sometimes be contentious. But when everybody involved follows a few guiding principles for successful performance reviews, the organisation can build employee trust and manager capability, both crucial ingredients for rewarding performance.

A pay framework

People want to feel that the rewards they receive are fair – fair in relation to three things: their performance or contribution; rewards their colleagues receive; and the reward package for similar work in other organisations. Without some form of pay framework it's difficult to explain why people are paid their current salary and opportunities for earning more. You don't need grades to do that, but you need to ensure people understand how they are paid.

Understanding your employment market: pay and benefits

Reward trends can change quickly, so it's important to know what the competition is up to. If you don't, employees certainly will. For many jobs, pay is sector specific and benefits are not. Benchmarking pay and benefits regularly enables the organisation to take informed decisions about the type and level of rewards which attract and retain the best people. It's an opportunity to find out what might make your organisation stand out from the crowd.

Equal pay

Your organisation's approach to equal pay says a lot about its commitment to equality and diversity, but "equality" shouldn't mean treating everybody in exactly the same way. For me, the key is "fairness" from the time people join, throughout their employment with the organisation and when they leave.

CHAPTER TWO
Rewarding performance

Case study

Special bonuses for special contributions at ABB Engineering Services

ABB Engineering Services (ABB ES) is a project-based engineering consultancy delivering solutions to major client organisations in the chemicals, pharmaceuticals, oil and gas industries. It makes extensive use of special bonuses for achievements in customer satisfaction, financial performance, personal effort and personal contribution. Its approach is summarised below.

Special bonuses are usually awarded to individuals as a result of excellent performance and commitment on a particular piece of work. This is assessed in terms of three factors: customer feedback; financial performance of the project; and personal contribution and effort made by the individual. Most bonus payments are between £450 and £1,000 although a few employees have received £2,000 to £2,500 for exceptional performance. Examples of individual achievements are set out below:

- Customer feedback on the outcome of the project

  - "Impressed by the performance of the ABB team and the commitment to delivery"
  - "Exceptional professionalism of the systems and people…probably the best I have seen in all my working years."
  - "Delight at the service provided…impressed by the developments in the service provided and the very positive attitude towards the work."

- Financial performance of the project

  - Higher profit margin than budgeted.

- **Personal contribution and effort**

  - Working long hours – average of 50 hours per week over 3 or more months, including weekend, bank holiday and shift working
  - Extended periods of travel away from home
  - A semi permanent secondment to another European location, resulting in substantial disruption to family life
  - Operating at a higher level role and being charged out at a higher fee rate for the whole of the year
  - "Excellent teamwork and determination"
  - Raising the international profile of a project.

To ensure consistency across ABB ES, special bonuses have to be agreed by a Business Manager (head of the business unit) and the General Manager and HR reviews and moderates all requests across the Company.

Rewarding performance
At a glance

Of course people believe rewards should match performance. The results of just about every employee opinion survey I've read tell me that. But there's a paradox here: why do the results also suggest that employees don't feel rewards match performance? Lack of funds, inadequate performance differentiation and poorly trained managers have a lot to do with it. But, the real reason may be much simpler. Perhaps most employees feel they're one of the higher performers and should be rewarded more.

Reward for performance whatever it's for – individual, team or organisational performance – is far from perfect and, of course, it never will be. But, The Together Company, unlike many other organisations I come across, is totally committed to making it work as "excellently" as possible. And it does so because it's the right thing to do for the business.[1]

Reward for performance is criticised on many fronts, much of which I disagree with profoundly. It favours blue-eyed employees – if that means good performers, I agree. When there's little difference in the pay of top and bottom performers, it hardly seems worthwhile. But my favourite criticism is…..giving two employees doing the same job a different pay increase causes resentment. That's very telling.

Some commentators – academics especially, but not exclusively – challenge one of the core assumptions about reward for performance. That is "people are motivated by money". They suggest that motivation is driven by non-financial factors, such as a challenging job or friendly work colleagues. I agree: these factors matter but they are not the only ones that affect motivation. A hotel receptionist's look of surprise when they are given an on-the-spot cash award of £30 or an afternoon off work, for "*going the extra mile*" for guests, says it all.

Most of the criticism misses the most important point about rewarding people. If they aren't rewarded for performance, what should they be rewarded for? I believe it's unacceptable to pay people more this year than last year just because they've turned up each day, irrespective of what they've achieved. However, there are many organisations that do. Perhaps they feel rewarding performance is too difficult to manage or that they can't differentiate between large numbers of people because there's little scope for performance variation in the work people do. That's fine when the annual, inflation-based base pay rise is accompanied by a variable pay plan that rewards employees for improvements, such as productivity, cost savings or customer satisfaction. But when it's not, this sends completely the wrong message to employees about what matters to the organisation's success, and ultimately, to their success. That's why rewarding performance matters a lot to The Together Company.

Four guiding principles for rewarding performance

My consulting work with clients tells me that rewarding performance succeeds only when it's based on four guiding principles:

- Focus on the few themes which will make a real difference
- Select the right framework
- Balance rewards for high performers and the vast majority of employees
- Ensure fairness at all times.

Guiding principle 1: Focus on the few themes which will make a real difference

One of my early recollections of working on rewards for performance with a client is that the project team identified 15 things that could make a real difference to the organisation. These included creating a high performance culture, increasing sales, reducing overhead costs, improving profit margins, being more innovative, increasing productivity, retaining our best people and varying pay costs according to the organisation's business results. While all these were important, the project team drowned in them and some of them were hardly SMART goals (Chapter 3, Performance management).

The key is to focus on those three to five themes which will really make a difference to the organisation's performance. These themes communicate to employees "what matters most" and are a unifying force for rewarding performance in different parts of The Together Company.

Guiding principle 2: Select the right framework

Rewards for performance can operate effectively at three broad levels – individual, team and organisation. The simple model in Figure 2.1 can help you identify the level at which rewarding performance might work best for your organisation.

FIGURE 2.1   Selecting the right framework

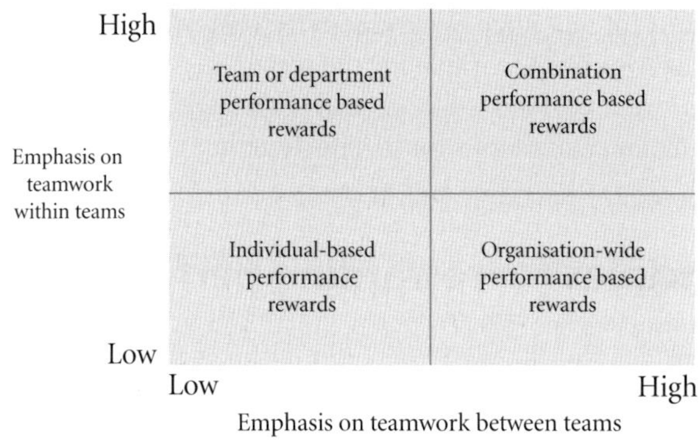

The model[2] is based on the importance attached to different aspects of teamwork in The Together Company and how these can be supported through reward. Four illustrative scenarios to think about in relation to your own organisation are set out below:

- If work is largely individually-based, where employees work largely independently of each other, rewarding individual performance makes sense.
- If teamwork within teams is crucial, for example at a retail bank branch, but there is little need for different teams to work closely together, team or department based rewards are likely to be the best approach.
- If co-operation between teams is vital, for example in a pharmaceutical company where the research and development and marketing teams need to work closely to bring commercially viable products to the marketplace, organisation based rewards may be the best option.
- If people within teams need to work closely and cooperation between teams is vital too, rewards linked to a combination of team, business unit and perhaps organisation performance would make most sense.

Guiding principle 3: Balance rewards for high performers and the vast majority of employees

I've met some senior executives who believe that linking reward and performance should be reserved for high performers only. Their belief is based on the assertion that "A players" contribute significantly more than "B performers" (some research evidence supports their view) so linking reward and performance for all employees is a waste of time. I'm a strong advocate of linking reward and performance and top performers should certainly receive top rewards that reflect their contribution, but focusing exclusively on these "A players" overlooks two important points about motivation and performance. First, it's de-motivational for the vast majority of employees on whom organisations ultimately rely. Second, the opportunity to raise the performance bar throughout the entire organisation is lost. Would you rather raise the performance of the top 5% of employees in your organisation from 85% to 90% or shift the performance curve for "effective performers", perhaps 75% of employees, from 60% to 65%? The answer, of course, is for you to decide!

Guiding principle 4: Ensure fairness at all times

Lack of trust and misunderstanding is the main reason for the failure of many schemes which reward performance. Too often this is because the process for rewarding performance isn't seen by those affected to be "fair" (the Concise Oxford Dictionary definition of "fair" includes the words "above board"). And if that's all employees, then that's a major problem!

Judged by the secrecy that surrounds many schemes I've seen, this feeling of "unfairness" is hardly surprising. But why should this be so? There are two reasons. First, part of employees' pay is potentially at risk and more often than not it's the downside risk, rather than the upside opportunity, that's of most concern to them. In an organisation which wants to replace its annual, cost-of-living based pay review with a performance-related pay review, employees may view this change as "unfair" because, potentially, it's a threat to their economic security.

Second, I come across many examples of performance based rewards which have been designed in isolation from the people who the plans are designed to motivate. So, even if there's a robust method for calculating rewards, employees simply mistrust the organisation's motives from the outset, because they weren't consulted in the first place. When that happens, there's little chance of achieving what the scheme set out to do. If it fails to deliver for employees, there's a very good chance it will fail to deliver for the organisation too.

But The Together Company knows that fairness is crucially important to successful performance related rewards, so when it's developing ideas for rewarding performance it consults employees by running a few focus groups, for example, to find out how employees feel about the idea. I recently did this for one of my clients, a small research company, where the employee opinion survey results said "pay is a dissatisfier". Early-on in the discussion it became clear that individually-based reward was viewed as "unfair" because most people worked to team or organisation objectives. Forty-five minutes later, there was near total agreement on which approach was going to resolve the pay issue and have employees' support – a combination of company-wide cash bonus and non-financial recognition of team achievements. To employees, this approach was "fair".

So, if your organisation has developed some ideas about rewarding performance, take employees into your confidence by telling them about your ideas, getting their reactions and having answers to the questions they are likely to ask. They need to be convinced that you have their interests at heart as well as those of the organisation and that the scheme will be operated fairly. Without that commitment to fairness, you'll be off to a rocky start.

But, for Together Companies, the initial commitment to fairness isn't enough; it knows it has to ensure fairness at all times and wherever it operates performance based reward. This means fairness in relation to four aspects:

- Putting the four principles described here into practice
- Establishing performance targets (Chapter 3, Performance management)
- Reviewing people's performance (Chapter 4, Fair performance review), and
- Distributing rewards (see below).

It requires business leaders who live up to their words and communicate regularly about how well the organisation, team or individual is doing in relation to performance targets. If projected rewards don't look like materialising because performance is below target, business leaders tell people promptly and why, and take action urgently to minimise the shortfall. After all, even if rewards are going to be lower than expected, it's far better to ensure the process is fair, than for employees to feel the process is unfair and to pay them less!

Resolving the five key design issues

Five key design issues have to be resolved in most schemes for rewarding performance. Here are some practical tips for doing so.

Design issue 1: Deciding what to measure – whats and hows

While there's usually little disagreement about linking reward and "what has been achieved" (outcomes / results) there's far less consensus about linking reward and "how outcomes have been achieved" (competencies, skills and behaviours). Why is this? Some people, of course, believe that only results matter. But I think there's another, more insightful reason for the lack of consensus. Many managers in particular are not comfortable with measuring competencies, skills and behaviours, and discussing these with the employee, so they focus entirely on outcomes / results. Others (including me) take the opposing view about the "hows" and believe they're important for one fundamental reason: what really matters is employees behaving in ways which are right for customers and long term growth of the organisation[3]. That's what leads to the desired outcomes.

I've no doubt, of course, that in some organisations (definitely not Together Companies I hasten to add) as long as employees achieve their performance targets, they can get away with upsetting customers, suppliers or work colleagues. But it won't be long before customers start voting with their feet and going to the competition, suppliers take their business elsewhere and team morale deteriorates.

The whats and the hows have to be measured, so a performance management framework which includes some form of competency assessment which managers and employees consider to be fair is essential (Chapter 3, Performance management).

Design issue 2: Deciding how to reward performance

There are two main ways of rewarding performance financially: through base pay and through bonus. I've seen both operate equally well. For The Together Company the decision comes down to which method will motivate employees in the desired manner and that may depend on the jobs they do and other opportunities for enhancing their earnings.

Base pay

This involves reviewing an employee's base pay in line with their performance (as judged through performance review) and deciding what, if any, pay increase should be awarded. The two main advantages of this approach (instead of a bonus) are that the employee "keeps" the award (base pay goes up) and it enhances other rewards, for example pension, which take account of base pay. From the organisation's point of view, however, base pay costs and the cost of rewards such as pensions rise at a faster rate than when a bonus is paid, because the bonus isn't consolidated into base pay. In most organisations base pay reviews take place annually, but there are some circumstances where a more frequent review might be appropriate, for example, where employees need to reach a required level of skill or competence after a defined time. One of my clients faced this issue, so in the first year of employment they made two uplifts in base pay which were linked to demonstrated improvement in skills / competencies after 3 and 6 months. In essence they rewarded the hows. A separate outcomes / results based bonus which was linked to team performance was awarded annually.

Frameworks for rewarding performance through base pay are presented in Chapter 5, A pay framework.

Bonus

The alternative to rewarding performance through base pay is to reward it through bonus. The main advantage claimed for employees is that they remember a bonus longer than an annual pay increase (that's questionable in my opinion) and, for the organisation, it's more cost effective because it's not consolidated into base pay and doesn't increase the cost of base pay-linked benefits. However, the fact that bonus payments aren't consolidated into base pay may mean employees prefer to receive performance related rewards in the form of an annual base pay increase. This way their base pay continues to rise, albeit not as fast as they might like on occasions.

The payment scale (for base pay or bonus) should be simple and show amounts at defined levels of performance. At its simplest, this might comprise three performance levels labelled "falls short of meeting objectives", "meets objectives" and "exceeds objectives" and a percentage of salary at each level. Concise examples of what is expected at each performance level can help inexperienced managers especially make informed judgments and go a long way to ensuring fairness and consistency. Other examples of performance rating scales are given in Chapter 4, Fair performance review.

Design issue 3: Deciding the degree of manager discretion over payments

One of the most important decisions to take is the degree of manager discretion over performance based rewards. Some organisations, especially those fairly new to performance based rewards, prefer to use a fixed percentage base pay increase or fixed bonus for a given performance level because this provides greater control over pay budgets. In other organisations, managers are given broad guidelines for making awards and they are expected to apply these fairly. The latter approach provides scope for rewarding variations in performance within broadly-defined levels, for example "meets objectives", where one employee only just meets them and another nearly exceeds them.

It's usually claimed that giving manager's discretion works best when performance management is embedded in the organisation and there's lots of experience of making performance based decisions about pay. No surprises there! However, it can be just as effective in very different circumstances. I recently helped a financial services client introduce a performance based reward plan for the first time in its history. Until then virtually everybody received the same, inflation based annual pay rise. By giving managers discretion over a range of base pay increases and issuing tough guidelines, the differentiation in rewards for high and low performers was far greater than envisaged at the start of the annual base pay review. The main reason was that manager's were "forced" to make performance based decisions about pay increases. They simply weren't allowed to revert to the previous approach. Very interestingly too, anecdotal evidence gathered at team meetings suggested that most employees were far happier with performance based rewards than the "everybody gets the same" approach.

Design issue 4: Deciding if bonus payments should be capped

I've sat down with business leaders of many clients and debated this issue. Sometimes they all feel strongly (perhaps like you) that the prospect of "exceptional rewards for exceptional performance" is a strong motivator, so the bonus scale shouldn't have a cap. On other occasions, opinion about capping payments is divided. But, if rewards for performance are designed to be self-funding (always a good principle) isn't a payment cap irrelevant?

Organisations that set a payment cap do so for two reasons. First, they want to manage peoples' expectations about bonus earnings. If the scheme has a good first year, employees may expect this to be repeated in the second and subsequent years, and (so the argument goes) they may be less inclined to strive for higher performance. When that happens employees are starting to feel "entitled" to the bonus. This should be strongly discouraged. The second reason for capping payments is that market conditions and trading performance change, sometimes unexpectedly, so the organisation prefers to err on the side of caution, rather than commit themselves to an open-ended payment scale which they may not be able to deliver. Capping has another advantage too. If performance is really exceptional, business leaders always have the discretion to make an additional award. The element of surprise can be a powerful motivator.

Design issue 5: Dealing with windfalls and shortfalls

There are times when business results are affected, adversely or favourably, by factors which might be considered to be "outside the control or influence of employees". Exchange rate fluctuations, a major customer going into liquidation or higher prices of goods and services, are possible reasons why business targets aren't met and rewards for performance are lower than expected. On the other hand, the sale of assets might result in a "profit windfall" which has little to do with the employees involved.

So, how should you handle these situations? To "automatically" say that all such factors will be included or excluded from the calculation of rewards is, in my opinion, hasty. A far better and fair approach is to consider, at the design stage, all the possible factors that can affect performance and rewards and decide which ones should be "genuinely excluded" and which should be "genuinely included". This can be achieved simply by having clear and unambiguous definitions of performance measures and the calculation of rewards.

Case study

Developing a new reward framework at Miller Insurance Services

Rewarding performance shouldn't stand in isolation from other reward practices – it should support and reinforce them. I've chosen this case study because it shows how rewarding performance fits into the total reward picture.

Miller Insurance Services Limited (Miller) is a specialist insurance and reinsurance broker, operating internationally and at Lloyd's. It is based in the City of London, and provides specialist risk transfer and consulting services for clients around the world. Founded in 1902, today Miller is the only remaining truly independent insurance and reinsurance broker of its size, based in the UK. Miller employs around 500 people.

Business Challenges

Miller faces challenging times on three fronts:

- Market: changing face of Lloyd's, globalisation of insurance markets and regulation by the Financial Services Authority
- People: recruitment and retention of key people, engendering drive and enthusiasm and changing people's mindset
- Organisational: maintaining profitability, giving clients greater value, enhancing Miller's reputation and attracting new business.

The Board knew that if Miller was to rise to these challenges, the business had to change. Miller already had a well-founded reputation for independence and the quality of its services, so the change needed to build on its current strengths, as summarised below.

Past	Future
• Transactional broker	• Client adviser
• Good at what we do	• Outstanding client service
• Few specialities	• Broad range of specialities
• Pockets of excellence	• Market leader in chosen specialities
• Value "production" above all else	• Value everybody for what they bring to and do for Miller
• Tendency to revert to "comfort zone"	• More innovative and proactive, step out of "comfort zone"
• Paternalistic - some protection from market turmoil	• Look after the right people for the right reasons - reward contribution
• Expectations of profit sharing	• Reward has to be "earned"
• Tendency to build personal empires and be protective	• Share clients and knowledge - have greater confidence in colleagues
• We go back over what we've decided	• More dynamism - learn from mistakes
• Tend to be cynical and blame	• Celebrate success / be positive
• Good/nice place to work	• Employer of choice

Developing the new reward framework

Miller's approach to pay and benefits had not kept pace with the change in the business, so it needed a fresh, business-focused approach that would help attract and retain talented people who were in short supply. Under the direction of Janet Oldham, HR Director, with consulting support from Strategic Reward, the company carried out a wide-ranging review of every aspect of pay and benefits – setting market-related salaries, annual salary progression, short-term incentives for all employees, long-term incentives for executives, benefits and work-life practices.

Following a series of discussions with each member of the Board and Business Unit Heads, and several employee focus groups, a set of reward principles were drawn up. These were:

- Align base salaries, incentives and benefits with the appropriate competitive pay market, which will be monitored regularly
- Link base salary review to the acquisition and demonstrated application of skills and qualifications and / or additional responsibility and / or individual performance
- Enable every employee to generate further earnings through incentives that are linked to individual performance objectives / targets and the financial success of Miller
- Provide a range and choice of benefits that reflect Miller's aim of being a "great place to work".

Several working groups were then set up to develop and evaluate potential reward practices. These took into account which rewards employees valued and the cost / benefit to both the company and employees. As the review progressed it became increasingly evident that, if Miller was to attract and retain the talented people it needed, action on several reward fronts was essential. Figure 2.2 summarises the changes.

Is it right for you?

Definitely! This isn't a matter of organisation size – rewarding performance is a core principle of Together Companies irrespective of organisational circumstances. As I've explored in this chapter, you have to decide the right framework for rewarding performance – for individuals, teams and the organisation as a whole – maybe all three. Not only that, you have to take decisions about the focus – the choices open to your organisation are set out in Part 2 of the book – Reward Choices. You should look at all four:

- **Rewarding team excellence**
- **Rewarding customer satisfaction**
- **Sharing financial success**
- **Rewarding business leaders.**

If you don't do the first three at the moment (hopefully you do have a coherent reward policy for rewarding business leaders!) my advice is select the reward practice

FIGURE 2.2   Reward change at Miller

Element	From	Towards
Base pay	• "I'm entitled to a pay increase each year" • Individual rates "negotiated" • Ad hoc sources of market data	• "My pay increase is linked to market data and my performance" • "I know what's expected of me" • Policy communicated to all employees • Specific salary and benefits • Surveys used for market data
Bonus	• Profit sharing "expected" by many senior people • Company bonus - everybody gets the same, irrespective of personal performance	• Senior management bonus related to company and individual achievements • Company bonus has individual performance element
Performance management	• Ad hoc – few guidelines, practices varied from good to indifferent • Annual chore for many managers – no structure for developing people	• Balanced scorecard to identify key drivers of company success and measure performance • Annual Performance and Development Review for all employees • Managers trained
Benefits	• Lots of slightly different packages led to inconsistencies over time	• Competitive, core package for all employees • Voluntary benefits being considered
Working arrangements	• Fixed, standard hours for everybody; little flexibility • Manage "presenteeism"	• Everybody is able to request (rather than be entitled to) flexible working • Manage contribution, irrespective of employees work-base
Reward communications	• People don't know financial value of their package – potentially undervalued	• Reward statements – salary, bonus and value of their benefits package

that's likely to have the most positive impact on business performance. So, if teamwork is poor, focus on rewarding team excellence – and don't forget the non-financial aspects too. Take a look at Chapter 13, Recognition and celebration for some ideas.

Key points

- People should be rewarded for performance, not just for turning up everyday.
- Focus on a few performance themes which will make a real difference – having too many measures is a common failing.
- Tailor rewards for performance to where they'll have the biggest positive impact on key performance themes – individuals, teams or your entire organisation.
- Use rewards for performance to raise the performance bar across all groups of employees, not just for high performers. That doesn't mean you shouldn't differentiate significantly when it's justified by performance – of course you should.
- When things go wrong, tinkering with the "mechanics" is not the answer, although it's a common response to a failing performance related reward plan.
- Manage payment expectations from the outset; beware the entitlement mentality.
- Give managers an appropriate degree of discretion over payments.
- Take employees with you – tell them about your plans for rewarding performance, gain their trust.
- Fairness, fairness and fairness – never, ever abandon it.

CHAPTER THREE
Performance management

At a glance

"The way we manage performance here is a complete waste of time. I don't have any input into my objectives and they're completely unachievable".

"At the start of the year I agree three or four key performance objectives with my manager. This gives me a clear focus and I know how my work fits into the department's business objectives".

These two, very different, views about performance management, sum up my consulting experience across many organisations. Why do views about performance management vary so widely? Why do managers and employees in some organisations feel it really works for them, while in others they go through the motions? The answer, quite simply, lies in the two quotes above. A top-down, imposed performance management process, introduced in "command and control fashion", isn't going to bring out the best qualities in people and produce the best results. It usually results in the opposite. But when people are involved in establishing their own objectives and coming up with ideas about how they can contribute to business objectives, they can "see what's in it for them". After all, people have practical experience of day-to-day work issues, so they often know what's realistic and what's not.

Performance management in The Together Company is about everybody taking responsibility for doing what matters most. It has three guiding principles:

1. It is owned and driven by line management, with support from HR
2. It is a process (not a system or package) that is developed specifically for the organisation. Although a common framework applies across the whole organisation, specific aspects of it, for example competencies, may vary by business unit, to reflect different business needs
3. It applies to all employees, not just business leaders.

Buy-in and commitment is therefore, far more about the "way" performance management is developed and introduced than it is about "design". That's not to say that a performance management process which has lots of forms and guidelines for completion (it looks and feels complex) isn't going to turn people off – of course it will. If people have been involved in the first place, simplifying the forms is easy; but if they haven't, gaining buy-in is an uphill task.

The performance management cycle

The terms used in performance management vary widely: performance agreements, work objectives, key performance indicators, competencies, performance development, personal development plans, coaching, mentoring, performance measurement, performance reviews, appraisals....the list goes on and on. Fundamentally, I believe that the different terms and parts of performance management can be grouped into three steps:

1. Planning: establishing performance objectives
2. Doing: working, day-to-day, towards achieving performance objectives
3. Reviewing: carrying out performance reviews and looking forward.

In The Together Company these three steps work as a continuous performance management cycle. Figure 5 shows the cycle at David Lloyd Leisure.

FIGURE 3.1   Performance Review Process at David Lloyd

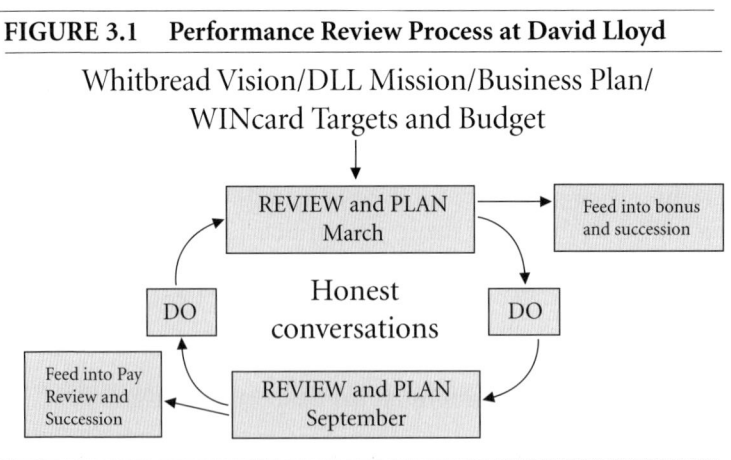

Whitbread Vision/DLL Mission/Business Plan/ WINcard Targets and Budget

---

The focus of this chapter is Step 1: Planning – establishing performance objectives. Step 2: Doing – which includes the personal development and coaching aspects of performance management – and Step 3: Reviewing, are closely linked and are major topics in their own right, so they are covered separately in Chapter 4, Fair performance review.

Establishing performance objectives: being SMART

There are two broad categories of performance objectives:

- What is to be achieved – these are the desired results / outcomes
- How it is to be achieved – this is the competence, skill, behaviour required to achieve the desired results / outcomes.

The process for establishing "what has to be achieved" usually starts at the business plan. But creating a clear line of sight between business objectives and the day-to-day work of employees is one of the toughest challenges facing organisations today. Giving different parts of your organisation considerable scope to translate organisation objectives into meaningful performance objectives for teams and individuals will go a long way to making them relevant to employees. In Chapter 1, The Together Company, we saw how David Lloyd Leisure deals with this challenge by translating the company WINcard into the Club WINcard. This gives employees clear focus for what matters most at their club level and everybody agrees with their manager how they will contribute to meeting WINcard performance targets.

But what is a meaningful or "good" performance objective? Objectives that are too easy to achieve have little effect on peoples' behaviour and lead to a culture of mediocrity and "second best". On the other hand, objectives that are nearly impossible to achieve are de-motivating and people see little benefit in trying to achieve them. People must believe they have a realistic chance of achieving and perhaps exceeding performance objectives. That's why Together Companies use the "SMART" model. Definitions of SMART vary: David Lloyd's version is below:

Specific	They should relate to one specific action
Measurable	You should be able to measure progress and success against the action
Agreed	They must be agreed between you and your manager
Realistic	They should be grounded in reality
Time Based	There is a time limit for the achievement of this action

Note the "one specific action" which gives the employee a very clear focus. Of course, SMART objectives must be described in language that people understand. In The Together Company the manager and employee sit down and agree how the employee can best contribute to team or department objectives, which in turn helps achieve the organisation's business objectives.

Agreement about objectives is crucial. Employees are far more committed to achieving performance objectives if they are actively involved in establishing them, rather than having them imposed by managers. Keeping a record of what's been agreed avoids potential misunderstandings later about what's expected from the employee and what support the manager will provide. The record can also help guide informal discussions about performance that take place from time to time.

I'm often asked how many objectives an individual employee should have, but there is no ideal number. The golden principle is that all of them should relate to those three to five themes which will really make a difference to the organisation's performance and avoid the trap of getting lost in minute detail to the extent that the main performance themes get lost. How employees are expected to achieve the 20-25 individual performance objectives that I see in many organisations, I shall never know.

So, what do SMART objectives in Together Companies look like? Some examples for a customer contact centre are set out below:

1. "Handle four customer enquiries per hour by the end of the month". This would be suitable for a new employee or all employees when overall performance has slipped below the minimum acceptable standard.

2. "Increase the number of customer enquiries dealt with satisfactorily first time, from 75% to 80%, by the end of the month". This would be suitable for everybody in the team, when customer satisfaction is not improving.

3. "Help employees identify opportunities for selling additional services, by coaching them in questioning and listening skills". This would be suitable for an experienced employee or a team leader.

4. "Develop a more reassuring telephone manner in the next two weeks". This would be suitable for a relatively new employee.

Objectives 1 and 2 are fairly straight forward because they are job-based. However, objectives 3 and 4 are potentially controversial because they are person-based and about competency, skill and behaviour. This is the "how" part of performance management, to which I turn next.

Encouraging appropriate behaviour – SMART competencies

This is about "how" results / outcomes are to be achieved – this is the competence, skill, behaviour required to do so. Some people say results / outcomes are all that matter; others, including myself and in most cases, customers too, believe that the way people do their job is important too. Contrast the great service you receive at one restaurant and the indifferent attitude of employees at another. It's obvious which one you'll return to!

Essentially competencies underlie the behaviours thought necessary to achieve a desired result / outcome. A competency is something you can demonstrate[1]. In this respect, competencies differ from knowledge, skill and expertise, which are the particular attributes a person requires to perform the various tasks associated with their role. However, when I use the term "competencies" I'm referring to "skills, competencies and behaviours". Admittedly, this definition is not for the purists, but it's grounded in practical experience of what organisations actually do. To encourage (and potentially reward) the competencies that lead to desired results / outcomes, the performance management process in many organisations incorporates competencies. To do so in your organisation, there are three things you have to get right:

- Selecting the right competencies
- Creating an easy-to-use competency framework; and
- Measuring the level of competence.

Selecting the right competencies

Deciding which competencies are right depends on what matters most to your organisation. Questions to answer include:

- What does the success of the organisation, perhaps its survival in the future, depend on?
- What specific behaviours do you need to encourage?
- Are there generic competencies common to all groups of employees as well as specific ones? If so, what are the different sets?
- Should you list the obvious – is it obvious to everybody?

Although there isn't an off-the-shelf set of competencies that can be universally applied or have been found to work more effectively than any other set, you don't have to start with a blank sheet of paper. By looking at what other organisations do and asking a representative cross section of employees in your organisation for their views about what might be appropriate, a short list can be drawn up relatively quickly. Types of competency and their definitions can vary enormously between organisations, so for ease of understanding, I've grouped all the different types and definitions of competencies into two broad categories:

General or core organisational competencies

These are the core competencies that everybody needs if The Together Company is to succeed. Examples include managing relationships, teamworking, planning and organising, decision making, influencing, personal drive and analysing information.

Job-specific competencies

These are competencies needed to succeed in a specific job or department. Examples include technical knowledge, business / customer awareness, team management, generating and building on ideas, and leadership.

Creating an easy-to-use competency framework

Many organisations combine core and job specific competencies in a single competency framework which applies to everybody. This creates a common language and understanding about what's valued.

> **A competency framework**
>
> A description of how people should work when delivering their performance objectives. It describes observable outcomes – the things you will see people doing.

I've seen lots of competency frameworks. Some are so complicated that they need pages of guidance notes to explain them. In contrast, competency frameworks in Together Companies satisfy the following criteria:

- Unambiguous
- Relevant to all people who will be affected by it
- Simple language (which reflects that used in the organisation)
- Discrete elements (no overlaps).

Each competency has a definition and several levels. In my experience, between four and eight competencies and three to six levels works well. Figure 3.2 shows a sample competency framework[2] comprising four competencies.

FIGURE 3.2   Overview of a sample competency framework

Competency	Dimension	Levels
Working with people	Managing relationships	Builds relationships internally Builds relationships externally Maintains external networks
	Teamworking	Is a team member Supports team members Provides direction for the team
	Influencing	Projects a positive image Influences the thinking of others Changes the opinions of others
Working with information	Gathering and analysing	Gathers and maintains information Checks and analyses information Uses information to analyse the business
	Decision making	Takes day-to-day decisions within set guidelines Takes more difficult decisions High-level decision making
Developing the business	People development	Develops self Develops others Develops a learning culture
	Ideas development	Takes active part in the generation of ideas Develops ideas into solutions Encourages an environment for developing ideas
Delivering results	Planning	Prioritises day-to-day workload Plans to meet departmental objectives Converts company plans into departmental plan
	Managing timescales	Takes responsibility for tasks Manages resources effectively

This framework also includes examples of actions at each competency level. So, for the competency "Working with people" and dimension "Teamworking", these are:

Level 1: Is a team member

Encourages colleagues to contribute in teams
Listens and gives credit to contributions made by colleagues
Shares knowledge with colleagues

Level 2: Supports team members

Encourages all team members to make useful contributions
Identifies when team members need support and provides it
Responds positively to the contributions of team members

Level 3: Provides direction for the team

Uses knowledge of individual's strengths, interests and development needs to delegate tasks
Provides regular feedback to the team about performance and business issues
Ensures that team members understand their individual and collective responsibilities

If the range and complexity of jobs in the organisation is diverse, generic competency definitions may need to be interpreted in the light of the specific job, such as senior manager or administrative assistant or a department. One of my clients – a hotel company – found this approach helped employees understand how competencies could work for them and explain what they needed to do to progress their career.

Not all organisations, however, approach the issue of "how objectives should be achieved" through a competency framework. Scottish Water is one such organisation which doesn't use the term "competencies" at all in its performance management process. People's commitment to achieving objectives in the right way is assessed against the company's four values – Involve People, Challenge for Benefit, Clear Conversation and Deliver Promises – which have been developed to include statements of positive and negative behaviour – Figure 3.3 is an example.

FIGURE 3.3   Scottish Water Value "Involve People": Examples of behaviour

Positive behaviour	Negative behaviour
• Uses feedback from others / team	• Responds negatively to others
• Treats people with dignity, respect and fairness	• Fails to listen to and involve others
• Listens to others and fairly considers all ideas and opinions	• Allows personal considerations to cloud judgments
• Helps others in the team on own initiative	• Doesn't consult people when appropriate
• Involves the team to produce optimum solutions	• Actively works in isolation
• Shares information openly	• Refuses to assist other team members in times of fluctuating workloads
• Raises issues and works with others to resolve them	• Keeps ideas to themselves and takes credit where it's not due
• Is open minded about different approaches to working	• Sticks to own ideas
• Recognises and takes account of the different strengths of team members	

This behavioural-based approach has been crucial in communicating to employees that, if the business was to succeed, what really mattered was how people behaved.

Measuring the level of competence

Once you've decided on an appropriate list of the right competencies and defined each one, the next step is to decide how you will measure people's competency against the definitions. In The Together Company, measurement takes place at the start of the performance management cycle to establish the current competency level and the target level, and at the end of the cycle to assess progress. Competencies can be measured in four main ways:

• Self assessment
• Manager's assessment
• 360 degree feedback; and
• Development centres.

I've excluded development centres from this book for two reasons: first, unless your organisation has only a handful of employees, it's impractical to put everybody through one and it's not needed for establishing SMART objectives and assessing performance; second, a discussion about development centres is more at home in a book about management development than it is in one about reward.

Self assessment

The Together Company involves employees in selecting the right competencies so it seems logical to include some sort of self assessment when measuring the level of competence. This can be done by a simple series of statements after each competency description, for example:

- I have difficulty doing this
- I sometimes have difficulty doing this
- I can usually do this
- I can always do this
- I don't need to do this.

This form of self assessment can be backed up with employee's records of examples and times when they've demonstrated particular competencies, such as teamwork, influencing or planning and organising. Keeping matters simple by recording a few representative factually-based instances is all that is needed.

Manager's assessment

This works like self assessment, with the manager using the list of competencies and definitions, and memory of the individual's performance during the review period to check what's been demonstrated. Frequency scales can help here too, for example:

- Never demonstrates
- Occasionally demonstrates
- Regularly demonstrates
- Nearly always demonstrates
- Always demonstrates.

It's normal practice in Together Companies for the manager's manager to check the assessment to ensure there are no glaring discrepancies between departments and individual managers.

360 degree feedback

The 360 degree aspect of performance review, discussed in Chapter 4, Fair performance review, applies here too. In my experience, a questionnaire-based approach is by far the best because it keeps matters factual and it's easy to administer. However, 360 degree feedback shouldn't be entered into without a great deal of careful thought. While it offers the chance of a more balanced view of competence than any one way of measuring it, everybody involved must be prepared to view the feedback constructively – and if the messages about performance aren't particularly positive, that can be tough!

Is it right for you?

While performance management is appropriate for all organisations, the approach used is likely to vary by organisational size, for example the number of employees and the way it's structured. Examples of approaches for different types of organisation are below.

Small but growing organisation

Clearly, your organisation doesn't want a complex process with an array of forms and rigid procedures. It needs a process that can grow from the normal management practices – assuming of course, that these are good practices. You could start with a presentation, given by the Leadership Team, to all employees explaining simply what your organisation is there to achieve, how it goes about it and how well it's doing. Time for questions and answers should be built-in. If it's impractical for everybody to attend one presentation, a couple of presentations may be required. The key points from the presentation could form the basis of a discussion between each manager and their team about how each person can best contribute to achieving your organisation's business objectives. The output from these discussions should be agreed performance objectives – definitely "what" and maybe "how". However, if "how" objectives are to be included, the process for measuring them must be simple and perceived to be fair.

Fairly large organisation

Your organisation is structured on a well-defined hierarchical basis, but the type of work and marketplaces differ markedly between parts of the business. This suggests that a one-size-fits-all performance management process is not suitable; however, you are keen to ensure a high level of consistency in the way performance management works throughout the organisation.

You could introduce a common performance management framework along the lines below:

- A cycle linked to the financial year for the entire organisation
- Objectives cascaded from the business plan for each part of your organisation. These could reflect common performance themes across all businesses. A balanced scorecard approach (see David Lloyd case study in Chapter 1, The Together Company) could work well here
- A set of core competencies that apply to everybody; plus specific business unit based competencies which are developed by each business unit.

Teams of senior managers could compare practices across business units by reviewing two key aspects of performance management: first, manager's and employee's feedback about how its working, gathered through a six-monthly survey; and, second, competency profiles – the current level and progress to the desired level of competency.

Project-team based organisation

Your organisation is based around projects and teams, where people move between different projects and may have several managers in a year. So, a project-based performance management process, where team and individual objectives are agreed at the start of the project and reviewed at the end, would make most sense.

You could incorporate competencies by having a framework based around customer needs, such as solutions, working relationships and business success, and incorporate important team competencies, such as knowledge sharing and encouraging colleagues. Personal development actions would be a natural outcome of each project and would emphasise project management and technical competency.

Business leaders could compare practices across projects along similar lines to those for a fairly large organisation, that is, feedback about how its working, gathered through a six-monthly survey and competency profiles – current and desired.

High-tech / professional services organisation

Your organisation is structured into departments, such as research and development, marketing, finance and customer / technical support. There's a strong focus on knowledge development and skills application, so a competency framework could feature strongly in your approach to performance management.

The framework could apply to everybody but because people's roles fall into two broad categories – technical and support – the competencies would be tailored to each generic role. Each person could have individual and team-based performance objectives, the mix depending on their role. The dynamic nature of the marketplace requires your organisation to respond quickly to changing customer requirements, so a quarterly update of performance objectives and personal development plans might be appropriate.

Key points

- Performance management isn't optional – it's at the heart of people management in Together Companies.
- Tailor the process to your organisation – focus on a few critical performance themes but vary the approach to reflect different business needs within the organisation.
- Make objectives SMART – specific, measurable, agreed, realistic and timed.
- Measuring "how" employees achieve performance objectives is often just as important as "what" they achieve. By incorporating objectives that relate to competencies / skills / behaviours your organisation creates a common language and understanding about what's valued.
- Agreement about objectives is crucial: people are far more committed to achieving objectives if they are actively involved in establishing them, rather than having them imposed by managers.
- Of vital importance is that people take the time and are committed to the performance management process, whatever that involves. When that happens, everybody wins. When it doesn't, everybody loses – and the business does too.

CHAPTER FOUR
Fair performance review

At a glance

Performance review always has been, and probably always will be, contentious. That's because it's highly personal, it's carried out by people and it doesn't always say the things people want to hear. But employees want to know how they are doing in relation to what's expected of them and how they can improve. If they improve, the organisation benefits too and that's central to the philosophy of The Together Company.

I've always believed in the principle "performance review should have no surprises". When there are surprises, managers and employees aren't communicating as often as they should be. Although an employee and manager may have different views about what's been achieved, the employee must feel that the review is fair and that it's based on performance during the whole period under review, not just an isolated incident, good or bad. Far too often people don't trust their manager to come to a reasoned and balanced view about what they've achieved. On the basis of the generalised statements I've seen in many appraisals, with little supporting evidence, I'm not surprised.

In addition, the length and complexity of some appraisal forms is mind-blowing, so the whole process becomes far too time-consuming, which hardly encourages people to take the time to evaluate performance thoroughly. There's another reason too – inadequately trained managers.

Finally, I don't like "performance appraisal" because, to me, it suggests a top-down process rather than the two-way responsibility I believe it should be. I prefer "performance review", so whenever I use this term I'm referring to appraisals, reviews, assessments and evaluations.

Performance review should be open, honest and fair

When performance review "goes wrong", nine times out of ten it's because feedback lacks credibility. It's too judgmental, lacks supporting evidence and is largely one-sided. Lack of clarity and agreement in the first place about what's expected gets people off to a bad start and failing to explain the impact on performance objectives, of changes in business priorities during the year, doesn't help.

Feedback can profoundly influence the way employees behave and the giving and receiving of feedback is one of the most significant ways of helping employees to develop personally and professionally in The Together Company. This brings me to the crux of successful performance review. It should be open, honest and fair. This is a two-way responsibility (Figure 4.1).

FIGURE 4.1   Performance feedback: A two-way responsibility

Responsibilities of the Reviewee	*Responsibilities of the Reviewer*
• Identify areas of responsibility which are unclear • Review performance regularly • Give early warning of problems that could result in failing to meet an objective • Gather feedback on performance from third parties, such as customers and colleagues • Have an honest discussion based on evidence of performance • Communicate clearly with manager • Suggest ideas for improving own effectiveness	• Ensure the individual understands what's expected of them • Align individual objectives with team / department and organisation objectives • Review performance regularly • Support, coach and give guidance to the individual on how to improve • Gather feedback on performance from third parties, such as customers and colleagues • Have an honest discussion based on evidence of performance • Recognise, reward and praise good work • Recognise under-performance and work with the individual to solve problems

---

Too often, feedback is associated only with the formal performance review that takes place annually in most organisations. But performance review shouldn't be seen just as an annual event. "Performance" is going on all the time, so it should be reviewed regularly. After all, organisations review their financial performance several times during the year, so why not employee performance too? That's why Together Companies encourage half-yearly or quarterly performance reviews and use informal feedback extensively.

Informal feedback

This is about the day-to-day exchanges between managers and employees, the informal chats over a cup of coffee or at lunch, or comments from a senior manager who drops into the department on a site visit. This, after all, is how it should be: managers and employees communicating regularly, discussing performance issues (good and bad) when they arise, rather than putting them off to a time when they've forgotten the detail and emotion takes over. Encouraging regular dialogue about performance minimises the risk of "surprises" too. In our busy daily lives at work, it's all too easy to forget informal feedback, but it's a powerful source of motivation even if the news isn't always good.

Formal feedback

This is feedback given at performance reviews and it can come from three main sources:

- The employee
- The manager
- Third parties, such as colleagues or customers.

Self review is important because it encourages the employee to take personal responsibility for their performance – and the behaviour and skills that help them achieve their performance objectives. Manager feedback is important because it's central to their role – to get the best out of an investment that often amounts to 40% of company costs.

Third party feedback is used because it offers an opportunity to obtain a more balanced view of performance than self review or manager only feedback sometimes achieves. Frequently referred to as "360 degree feedback", third party feedback involves tapping into the views of a wide cross-section of people, such as team colleagues, people in other departments and external contacts for example, customers or suppliers, who have regular contact with the employee or the team if team performance is being reviewed.

For organisations which currently use manager-employee only reviews getting feedback from all these additional sources may sound daunting, but it doesn't have to be. Simply asking team colleagues for their views is a good starting point and this often makes the employee feel they are being reviewed by people who really understand their job and the contribution they make – I know the manager should! Taking things one-step at a time is far better than moving immediately from manager-employee review to full 360 degree feedback before some of the basic feedback mechanisms, for example questionnaires, have been tried and tested.

> **360 degree feedback**
>
> The collection and feedback of performance data on an individual or group, obtained from several sources such as peers, team members, manager, internal customers and external customers / contacts.

360 degree feedback, like any other feedback of course, must be credible. The Together Company achieves this in two ways. First, by asking relevant and timely questions and obtaining concrete examples of good performance and suggestions about how performance could be further improved. This avoids so-called "personality issues". Second, by maintaining anonymity, that is not naming the specific source of feedback, whenever possible. This avoids potentially damaging personal conflict if feedback, especially negative, is linked to named sources. However, there may be some occasions when naming the specific source is important, for example, when the employee has done a great job for a customer or when things need improving rapidly.

Three guiding principles for successful performance reviews

To ensure that performance review is open, honest and fair, The Together Company keeps to three guiding principles:

- Prepare thoroughly
- Question and listen; and
- Give constructive feedback.

Guiding principle 1: Prepare thoroughly

When people are ill-prepared for a discussion about performance it shows visibly. The manager has very little to say other than "everything seems fine to me so just carry-on as you are" and there is little opportunity for the employee to discuss the issues that really matter to them. Similarly, the employee appears disinterested, asks few questions and doesn't want to make any effort to improve. When these situations arise, the entire discussion is a waste of time.

Preparation starts with adequate notice of the discussion time, place and agenda. At least one week's notice should be given, not 24 hours that I come across in many organisations. Booking a quiet and private location, free from interruptions and allowing sufficient time are essential too. The 10-point check list in Figure 4.2 (which can be modified easily for the Reviewee) should ensure you get the best out of the meeting.

FIGURE 4.2   Performance Review: 10 point check-list

1. How well has the employee achieved his / her objectives during the review period?
2. How well have any training plans or development agreed at the last review meeting been put into practice?
3. What objectives would you like to agree with the employee for the next review period? This may require a separate ad-hoc meeting.
4. Has the employee had any problems in carrying out his / her work? If so, what sort of problems and what can be done about them?
5. How satisfied are you that you have given the employee sufficient guidance, help or coaching on what he / she is expected to do? What extra could you provide?
6. Is the best use being made of the employee's skills and abilities? If not, what should be done?
7. Is the employee ready to take on additional responsibilities in his / her present job? If so, what?
8. Do you think the employee and the organisation would benefit if he / she were provided with further experience in other areas of work? If so, which?
9. What direction do you think the employee's career could take within the organisation?
10. What development or training does the employee need to help in his / her work and to further develop their career with the organisation?

Guiding principle 2: Question and listen

Now it's time to put the preparation to the test – the performance review discussion. How long should the meeting last? The answer is: "As long as it takes to cover all the points in the preparation list". In my experience, around one to two hours is about right. If this turns out to be inadequate, because lots of unforeseen issues or major differences of opinion emerge, it may be better to meet again. If this happens it's important to have a clearly defined and agreed agenda and outcome for the second meeting. Going over old ground won't move the discussion forward.

If the manager and the employee are to contribute fully to the performance review discussion they must ask the right questions and be good listeners. Figure 4.3 gives some helpful and unhelpful questions.

FIGURE 4.3 Performance discussion: Helpful & unhelpful questions	
Helpful questions	*Unhelpful questions*
● **Open** questions encourage the flow of information. They generally begin with: What, Why, Where, How, Tell me about. ● **Closed** questions are direct and focused, calling for a straight and simple answer. They often require a "yes" or "no" response. They control the flow of information. ● **Probing** questions are used to follow up answers and obtain more detail. They are extremely useful and require attentive listening. They aim for depth rather than breadth. ● **Linking** questions or statements provide summaries to confirm understanding and make transition to new topics. They help maintain a steady pace and rapport.	● **Leading** questions are directive, indicating the preferred answer. They could begin with "surely, you agree….?" They are not productive in obtaining depth and quality of information. Their use should be limited otherwise the discussion will become dominated by the manager. ● **Multiple** questions are several questions joined in a series. They tend to be confusing and therefore produce limited information. They're normally used when the manager hasn't clearly planned the questions. They can allow the individual to choose to answer only one of the questions. The manager then needs to follow up using probing questions which will be much more effective.

Active listening is an important skill for managers in The Together Company. Listening to the employee's views and concerns and really understanding their career aspirations are key attributes of a good manager, and employees notice them. Listening is important also for the employee who's receiving feedback. Too often, misunderstanding about performance achievements arises because people don't really "listen" to what's being said. They latch onto a few words and jump to the wrong conclusion, without checking their understanding. So, remember the word LISTEN as described in Figure 4.4 and the key points from each of the six letters.

FIGURE 4.4	Listening	
L	Look interested	Show encouragement Use eye contact to maintain rapport Stay relaxed, maintain an open position and don't fidget
I	Inquire with questions	Use open, closed, probing and linking questions
S	Stay on target	Keep to the point – remember the aims of the discussion
T	Test understanding	Restate to ensure understanding – "so, are you saying…? Summarise at intervals
E	Evaluate the message	Observe the individual's behaviour – is it consistent with the words?
N	Neutralise feelings	Stay calm, retain self control and keep an open mind

Guiding principle 3: Give constructive feedback

Giving feedback doesn't come easily to many managers or employees, but by following a few simple guidelines even those who lack confidence are often surprised to find it's not as daunting as they thought it was going to be. The key is to be constructive (Figure 4.5).

FIGURE 4.5 Constructive Feedback: Guidelines	
Giving Feedback	*Receiving Feedback*
• **Be helpful:** don't hurt or deflate, always be constructive • **Be open and direct:** deal with specific behaviour or incidents, both positive and negative • **Express feelings:** convey how you feel about performance, not just a bald statement of facts, so employees can judge the full impact of your views • **Discuss options:** Ask for and discuss alternative ways of behaving which allow the employee to think about new ways of tackling old problems • **Actions:** summarise your understanding of the feedback you have given and agree how this will be used.	• **Listen to the feedback:** it can provide useful insights about you and your effectiveness • **Be clear about what is being said:** be sure you understand the comment before you react to it. "So, you are saying that….." Ask for specific examples of behaviour or incidents, both positive and negative • **Discuss options:** test what might have been a better way by putting forward your own ideas and asking your manager for his / her reaction • **Think about it:** you may not always agree with what you hear, but don't dismiss it out of hand. Be prepared to discuss it further • **Actions:** summarise your understanding of the feedback you have received and agree how you will use the feedback.

Performance rating

This is one of the most controversial aspects of performance review. Fairness is critically important here and the lack of it is usually the heart of any controversy. The key question is: Should you have a rating scale?

The argument for rating

The most common argument for rating is that it's not possible to take decisions about performance and reward without it. Of course it's "possible": the issue is whether such decisions are considered to be useful and fair, hence the need for some form of structure or rating.

While it's impossible to prevent a manager and an employee holding different views about what's been achieved and how well, performance rating, backed up with clear definitions and examples of different levels of performance, can help communicate particularly difficult messages to under-performers – and particularly positive ones to outstanding performers as well.

Rating also provides a basis for predicting potential on the assumption that people who perform well in their present job are likely to go on doing well in the future. However, this may be the case only when there are elements of the present job which are important in a higher level or different job too. Examples of such elements are judgment, influencing and drive that feature in Whitbread's career / potential assessment of managers (David Lloyd case study, Chapter 1).

The argument against rating

The counter view about performance rating is that it reduces performance review to a simplistic box-ticking exercise. When it does – and I've seen this happen on too many occasions – people end up "going through the motions" and the value of an open, honest and fair discussion is destroyed. Some organisations use individual descriptions of what's been achieved (or not) rather than rating, because they believe this leads to more informed judgments about reward and career development.

However, when it comes to dealing with under-performance, rating or no rating, ducking the issue shouldn't be tolerated.

I've seen rating and non-rating work extremely well in the same type of organisation. This comes down to culture more than the so-called "rights and wrongs" of rating. The number one aim of The Together Company is joint agreement between manager and employee about performance achievement in relation to the objectives agreed at the start of the review period and what needs to happen in future. If you believe rating helps frame those discussions and subsequent decisions about pay (my experience tells me it often does on both counts) then use it. If you believe it doesn't, then don't.

Rating scales

Rating scales don't have to be complex – in fact the simpler the better is a good maxim. They tend to fall into two categories: positively-defined; and positive-to-negative. Figure 4.6 shows a four-level, positively defined rating scale[1].

FIGURE 4.6   Four-level, positive rating scale

Rating	Criteria
1	Meets basic standards of the role, although several objectives are not met and there is considerable room for improvement
2	Most objectives are met to required standard, some areas need improvement
3	Exceeds some objectives, meets all others
4	Exceeds all objectives, consistently performs beyond normal requirements

Positively defined rating scales seek to avoid the use of terms for middle-ranking performers, such as "acceptable", "satisfactory" or "competent" which can seem to be giving faint praise. However, the alternative rating scale – positive to negative – doesn't have to convey this impression, as the performance rating guidelines at David Lloyd Leisure show (Figure 4.7).

FIGURE 4.7   David Lloyd: Performance rating guidelines for Club Team Members

Rating	Criteria
O – Outstanding	A level of phenomenal performance, which is considered far above what is expected of the role. Outstanding skills and abilities are displayed consistently.
E – Exceeding	A level of performance that is well above what is expected of the role. Skills and abilities above our expectations are displayed consistently.
A – Achieving	Achieved the high level of performance that is expected of the role. Development tasks have been met and achieved consistently.
G – Growing	A level of performance where the team member is showing consistent improvement achieving some, but maybe not all of the key tasks. Likely to be applied in the first six months of job.
U – Unacceptable	This reflects a level of performance where key tasks have not been achieved and without consistent improvement.

The language used in rating scales – impersonal numbers, wordy definitions or a simple sentence – can be highly emotive. I don't have a preferred rating "language" because I've seen all types work equally well. The decision about which to adopt is simply down to what fits your culture.

There's been much debate about what comprises the "best" number of ratings levels, but I don't believe it exists. Experience has told me that a minimum of three and maximum of six rating levels is practical. Differentiation between more than six levels requires very precise level definitions and I doubt the majority of people are able to make those differentiations easily, let alone defend their usefulness.

Achieving consistency

The problem with rating scales is that it's very difficult to ensure that a consistent approach is adopted by all managers. Some managers will be more generous or harder than others. The Together Company deals with this issue in two ways:

- Defining the expected distribution of performance ratings – forced or unforced
- Through training and monitoring.

Performance distributions

Many organisations believe, rightly in my opinion, that it's highly unlikely that all employees in the same department could be justifiably classed as Excellent, for example, so they define an expected distribution of performance ratings[2]. One of the most commonly used distributions conforms to the "normal distribution" which for a five-point scale might translate into 5/15/60/15/5. For the normal distribution principle to work there needs to be 50 or more employees. Departments with fewer than 50 employees should be combined for the purpose of comparing actual and expected performance distributions.

However, there's no rule which states that performance should be normally distributed in an organisation. I've come across many examples of organisations where key departments, such as sales or research and development, have more than their "normal share" of above average people and other departments which don't. In these circumstances, a skewed distribution of 10/40/30/15/5 for example, may be more appropriate. One organisation I know has a 10/85/5 distribution. What performance distribution would you expect in your organisation?

Forced-distribution versus unforced distribution

For many organisations, the performance distribution is a guideline (that is "unforced") and ratings are challenged if the distribution is out of line with that expected. These organisations believe that educating and training managers in performance review is a far better approach than forcing ratings into a distribution which might be acceptable this year but not the next, because what really matters is performance improvement. While it's perfectly possible, of course, to change the distribution each year, it's not an approach to be adopted lightly. It requires a business rationale which is simple and easy to explain to everybody and that's where the difficulty lies.

However, there are organisations that believe the unforced approach simply doesn't work and is an excuse for avoiding poor performance in particular. But, any attempt to impose a distribution (a forced distribution) to ensure consistency is often controversial and opens up new issues to do with fairness.

A forced-distribution, from an organisation standpoint, allows easier allocation of performance-related reward budgets but that's hardly going to go down well with those employees whose rating is changed because (in their eyes) it doesn't fit the company's pay budget model. Not only that, individual ratings can't be definitively known at the time of the performance review because all performance ratings need to be compared and the initial ratings may change as a result of the comparison.

It's perfectly reasonable for employees to want to know (and be given) at the time of performance review, a firm indication of how well they have performed. If that initial rating changes when the forced-distribution is applied, they should be given a full and open explanation of why. This puts managers on the spot and some may be inclined to give little away at the performance review discussion or talk in very general terms. That alone, may make some employees feel that their manager is hiding something and when this happens the core principle of "open, honest and fair" performance reviews is seriously compromised. In my view, "honesty is the best policy" and the manager should give their views about the employee's performance, fully supported with evidence, but with the appropriate caveat about the final rating. Rating changes should occur only when the performance is border line and affect only a few employees. If they occur more frequently, it's time to find out why. Refresher training in performance review may be the answer.

Training and monitoring

The second way The Together Company strives to achieve consistency is through training and evaluation. It runs workshops with managers from different departments to discuss how performance ratings are perceived, to explore differences and test fair ratings on case examples. Running workshops at regular intervals helps build-up a common view and level of comfort with the performance rating process. Managers might also meet after the performance review discussions and initial ratings to exchange information and, where necessary, justify their distribution of ratings (often referred to as "calibration"). Requiring a manager's manager to check on the quality of performance reviews and the consistency of rating should be part of the process too.

Simple and easy-to-complete documentation

When the documentation looks complicated performance review can be viewed as an uphill task – irrespective of the merits of the approach. But simple documentation isn't difficult to achieve, as the performance review form at David Lloyd illustrates. Figures 4.8 and 4.9 are extracts from two sections called "How was it for you" and "My Self Assessment" which answer everything that's needed in performance review – past performance assessment and future development for the team member.

With today's technology of course, the form filling can be completed electronically.

Is it right for you?

While fair performance review is appropriate for all organisations, the approach used is likely to vary by organisational size, for example the number of employees and the way it's structured. Examples of approaches for different types of organisation are below.

Small but growing organisation

Just like the process for establishing performance objectives should be simple (see "Is it right for you?" in Chapter 3, Performance management) performance review should be simple too. However, if it's too simple, employees may question management's commitment to the process. You could have something along the following lines:

- A four-page form: brief description of why performance review is important to the organisation and what's in it for employees; some key tips for the reviewer and the reviewee – these could be drawn from Figures 4.2, 4.3, 4.4 & 4.5; a review of performance over the last performance period; and the final page for objectives over the next performance period and career development / training actions.
- Carried out annually; perhaps giving employees the option to have a six-monthly progress review.
- Start with self review – should be strongly encouraged – and manager review.

FIGURE 4.8 David Lloyd Leisure "How was it for you?" (extract)

Team member to complete and return to your manager at least three days before the review.

1. What aspects of your work have given you the most satisfaction during the past year, and why?

5. What might help you do your job more effectively, e.g. training equipment, help from your manager, and why?

2. Was there anything you feel did not go so well, and why?

6. Are there any actions agreed at your last review which have not yet been completed? If so, what are they?

3. Has your current job changed much over the last year and if so how?

7. How have you actively inspired our members and contributed to our WINcard?

4. What are the areas you would like to build on in the coming year?

8. Looking ahead, what would you like to discuss regarding your career development?

- Taking on another role ☐
- Learning a new role, but retaining your current one (multiskilling) ☐
- More responsibility ☐
- I am happy in my current role ☐

FIGURE 4.9 David Lloyd Leisure "My Self Assessment" (extract)

Team member to complete and return to your manager at least three days before the review.

Give yourself a rating on the following areas. Simply tick one box in each section and add any further comments in the top section of the box on the right. (The actions and timescales will be agreed at your review meeting with your line manager).

Job knowledge

☺ Extremely competent in all aspects of the job. Understands and carries out all accountabilities and routines.

☺ Well informed about the job and procedures.

😐 Good understanding of the job.

☹ Lacks knowledge in several key areas.

☹ Lacks minimum knowledge/skills to perform job.

Team member comments		
Agreed actions	Timescale	Who is responsible

Reliability

☺ Completely reliable. Finishes a job every time.

☺ Above average dependability. Usually persists with job or task

😐 Trustworthy and reliable. Good level of persistence.

☹ Sometimes unrealizable. satisfied to 'get by'.

☹ Often unreliable. Does not assume responsibility.

Team member comments		
Agreed actions	Timescale	Who is responsible

When you discuss your agreed actions with your manager you will need to ensure that they are SMART

SMART	
Specific	They must relate to one specific action.
Measurable	You should be able to measure progress and success against the action.
Agreed	They must be agreed between you and your manager.
Realistic	They should be grounded in reality.
Time Based	There is a time for the achievement of this action.

Fairly large organisation

If you can manage with the four-page form suggested above for the small organisation, that's fine. But if your performance management process incorporates a competency framework it's likely that a longer form, say eight pages, will be required. This could comprise the following sections:

- Guidance notes for the reviewer and the reviewee – what's in it for everybody
- Review of past performance – referring to current objectives
- Competency definitions – these might be a summary of what's described in the full competency framework
- Agreed objectives for the next performance period
- Career development / potential review with agreed personal development plan.

Self assessment and manager assessment should be mandatory – and that should go for competencies too. Business leaders of each part of the organisation could have discretion to introduce 360 degree feedback.

Project based / high tech / professional services organisation

The performance review form could be very similar to that described above for the large organisation. Self assessment, manager assessment and customer feedback about performance would apply to everybody. Personal development actions would be a natural outcome of each project and would emphasise project management and technical competency. End of year performance reviews would reflect achievements throughout the year and consider any special contributions, for example developing a standard proposal template which was based on successful bids to win customers.

Keeping up to date with changes in customer requirements may make a quarterly performance review appropriate. You might also introduce a Career Counsellor for everybody (who might not necessarily be the employee's manager) to help them develop their career.

Key points

- Good performance reviews don't have surprises for individuals or managers.
- Clarity and agreement in the first place about what's expected gets everybody off to a good start.
- Performance reviews are a two-way responsibility.
- Encourage regular dialogue about performance throughout the year: regular informal feedback and discussion helps keep everybody on track to achieving what matters most.
- Performance feedback is one of the most significant ways of helping employees to develop personally and professionally. Tell things as you see them and illustrate this with concrete examples and guidance for improvement.
- Incorporate third party feedback – colleagues, direct reports, customers – when appropriate. It can help achieve a balanced view of performance.
- Prepare thoroughly, question and listen, and give constructive feedback – and that's a two-way responsibility.
- Rating scales aren't compulsory! But they can help achieve consistency and that's essential. Scales don't have to be complex – the simpler the better.
- Train everybody to deliver fair performance reviews and monitor progress by asking their opinion.

CHAPTER FIVE
A pay framework

Managing Pay at Manchester United

A recent Staff Satisfaction Survey at the club highlighted Reward & Recognition as a priority for improvement. Working with Anthony Lawler, Head of Human Resources and his team, Strategic Reward helped Manchester United develop a total reward strategy (Figure 5.1) which has three principal components:

- Compensation (Pay)
- Benefits
- The Work Experience

This case study looks at the compensation (pay) aspects in particular.

Pay framework

Manchester United doesn't operate a formal job evaluation process or have formal pay bands which have been determined as a result of such a process. It's chosen this approach for one key reason, as Anthony Lawler explains:

"Our business is very diverse and we already have well established job structures and recognised jobs in most parts of it, which we benchmark in the relevant employment markets to ensure we provide competitive salaries, so a formal job evaluated structure and associated pay bands wouldn't offer any additional advantages. In fact, the current flexible approach is absolutely essential to attracting and retaining key talent across all parts of our business."

However, in the light of the Staff Satisfaction Survey findings, it was clear that employees didn't understand how their annual salary review increases were determined. As a result of this feedback, the Club decided to implement some changes to the pay award process. These were designed to build a fairer, clearer system for reviewing pay increases and to reward individual performance. The previous process had two components – base pay review and profit share bonus; the new process has four components which are shown below:

- **Basic pay review:** all employees receive the same % increase to basic salaries.
- **Additional rise for extra responsibility:** managers may award an additional amount to recognise significant changes to an employee's job or responsibilities, or where employees have substantially developed themselves to such an extent that there is a significant improvement in the contributions that they have made to the business. Positive examples of knowledge, skills and behaviours in the workplace, in areas such as customer service and relationships, team working, challenges to improve, creativity and innovation, drive, commercial awareness and "develops others", help inform this assessment.
- **Individual performance bonus:** an additional sum of money is made available to reward and recognise outstanding contribution during the year. It is designed to recognise the part that individual employees play in the achievement of business goals and living the vision and values. There are two categories of award:

  - Going the extra mile – up to £5,000 for performance delivery in a key project, one-off responsibility in addition to normal responsibilities or revenue/savings generating activity. This award goes to a very small number of employees.
  - High performance – £1,000 for consistent outstanding performance throughout the year or excellent business awareness visible through what they have achieved.

Nominations for a one-off, individual performance bonus payment are made by the relevant Executive Director and approved by a Central Remuneration Panel consisting of Executive Directors and the Head of HR, and chaired by the Chief Executive.

- **Staff profit share bonus:** the Company operates a staff profit share bonus which is designed to reward the permanent staff of Manchester United with annual bonuses in years when the company achieves a high level of profitability. In particular, years when there are "cup" successes, for example the FA Cup or European Cup (involving all staff in organising and staging matches) are likely to produce a higher level of profitability. 2.5% of the actual operating profit above budget is distributed to all full time and permanent part-time employees, as a percentage of salary.

The HR Team has worked hard at communicating the new pay approach as part of the Total Reward Strategy. It will be interesting to see how employees feel about the new process when they take part in the next Staff Satisfaction Survey.

Figure 5.1 Manchester United: Total Reward Strategy

Vision: To be the best football club in the world both on and off the pitch

Values: Incorporate how we intend to operate on a day to day basis, they are at the heart of everything we do, they are a mix of the traditional behaviours that have built Manchester United into what it is today, a successful and professionally run football club.

Our values are represented by the following acronym:

United…with our fans in our commitment and passion for the club
Non-discriminatory…in making Manchester United accessible to all, irrespective of age, race, gender, creed or physical ability
Innovative…in our ambition to be "first to the ball" at all times
Team-orientated…in our desire to work together with the same dedication displayed in every game by our first team squad
Excelling…in our aim to be world-class in everything we do
Determined…in our pursuit of success while being accountable for our actions.

Compensation
- Base pay review
- Additional Rise to Recognise Extra Responsibility
- One-off Bonus for Outstanding Contribution during the Year
- Manchester United Staff Profit Share Bonus

Benefits
- Pension scheme
- Life cover
- Holidays
- Sick pay
- Company negotiated discounts
- Other contractual benefits, including
    - BUPA cover
    - Company car
    - Mobile phone
- Staff restaurant

The Work Experience
- Acknowledgment/appreciation/recognition
  - Employee of the Month (VVIP) / Year Awards
  - Service Recognition (including opportunities to purchase match tickets)
  - Social Events (Party on the Pitch, Christmas Party)
  - Performance Reviews
- Balance of work and life
  - Part-time work initiatives
  - Sports and Social club
- Culture
  - Vision & Values
  - Communications (including RedLines, monthly departmental briefings)
  - Reward & Recognition of Performance
- Staff development
  - Performance and Development Review
  - Company sponsored training / qualifications
  - Career Progression
  - Self Improvement
  - Leadership Development
- Environment
  - Facilities (work stations / equipment, staff rooms / kitchens)
  - Place of Work (Stadium Buildings, Carrington & Cliff)
  - Health & Safety Provisions

At a glance

Pay structures are the past, rather than the future. Pay structures do more harm than good. Provocative statements – certainly! Ill-founded ones – definitely not! Just talk to your peers in smoke-stack traditional industries with trades unions sitting around a table discussing pay and grading, and ask them how they feel. They know how difficult it is to change pay structures that have been in place for several years and the entrenched attitudes that go with them.

Too often discussions about pay structures get submerged in the detail rather than the reasons why some form of pay structure might be appropriate. I prefer the term "pay framework" because pay structure often implies lots of grades and bureaucracy but, as we saw at Manchester United, it doesn't have to be that way.

The first question to answer is: "Why do you need a pay framework?" The answer is: "Because you need to communicate the basis for paying people". You don't need grades to do that, but you do need to ensure employees understand how their pay is determined and reviewed.

When the organisation has a small number of people, ad hoc, individually negotiated approaches to pay are usually the order of the day. But as the organisation grows, people want to gain new experience and develop their skills. They get to know what their colleagues are earning too. Without some form of pay framework, it's difficult to explain why they're paid what they are and opportunities for earning more.

The pay framework in The Together Company does two things which help to motivate and retain talented people. These are:

- Provide a logical basis for making fair and consistent decisions about pay levels, pay progression and differentials on the basis of employee performance / contribution, skill / competence and job size
- Help reconcile often conflicting demands for internal equity and market competitiveness.

Most importantly, the pay framework fits the circumstances and culture of The Together Company, so, it operates flexibly in a fast-moving business environment for example, or is rigorously applied where order matters most.

Types of pay framework

There are four main types of pay frameworks open to The Together Company: individual pay bands or spot rates, grades, broad bands and job families. Figure 5.2 summarises their key features, advantages and disadvantages[1].

Although this may help narrow the choices about which framework might be most appropriate for your organisation, your final decision must take into account two important factors:

- Your attitude to job evaluation
- The desirability of pay bands and how you feel people's pay should progress.

Job evaluation

The pros and cons of job evaluation have been debated for decades, but fundamentally, job evaluation is a process for determining the relative worth of jobs in an organisation – and no organisation can avoid it. That's because it's impossible

FIGURE 5.2 Pay frameworks for The Together Company

Framework	Brief description	Advantages	Disadvantages
Individual pay bands or spot rates	A single rate or separate pay band for each job. Relativities between jobs are usually determined either by market rates or job evaluation.	Avoids problem of grouping several jobs with widely different sizes into a grade. Pay band easily changed in response to market pay movements.	Can encourage individuals to push for job re-grading. Can be more difficult to control than conventional graded structures. Heavy to administer.
Grades	A sequence of job grades each with a pay band. Bands have a market reference point and often overlap. Jobs are allocated to grades on the basis of their relative size, which is determined through job evaluation.	Easy to explain to employees. Consistent method of grading jobs. Individuals can be moved to jobs of slightly different sizes without the need to change pay.	Grade boundaries can cause friction. Tendency for grade drift. Grouping different sized jobs into one grade may lead to some being over-paid or under-paid.
Broad bands	The range of pay in a band is significantly higher than in a conventional graded structure. Usually cover all employees. Each band usually has a number of pay zones for specific groups of jobs.	Reduces grade drift problem. Flexibility in pay decisions. More authority devolved to managers. Flexibility to appoint people to different roles without need to change pay.	Balancing control over pay decisions and fairness not achieved easily. Rigorous tracking of market rates – but often not the most rigorous! Lots of hands-on guidance required.
Job families	A separate framework for each job family (e.g. Finance, Marketing, HR, IT). Jobs in each family are related in terms of basic skill but are differentiated by level of responsibility. Each job family is aligned to market rates and contains several pay bands which reflect different levels of work.	Suitable when groups of jobs need to be treated differently due to the nature of their work and market rates vary by job group.	Can be divisive and internal equity may be more difficult to achieve. Great care needed to justify different treatment of some jobs.

to avoid making decisions about pay and, if they're not negotiated, pay decisions will be made on assumptions about where the job fits into the organisation, the performance of people and the market rate for the job or the person. The key issue is whether an organisation should have a "formal" job evaluation process. The arguments, for and against, are summarised below.

Arguments in favour

- It can help to produce order out of the chaos that exists in organisations which have allowed pay decisions to be made in an entirely ad hoc and subjective way.
- Equal pay for work of equal value can be achieved only through the use of formal analytical methods of job evaluation.
- A formal process is more likely to be accepted as fair than an informal or ad hoc process and is more transparent.

Arguments against

- Inflexible in reacting to business and work changes
- May ignore market forces, although standardised job evaluation supports robust benchmarking
- Its focus is jobs, not people (competence-based approaches help overcome this criticism)
- Too time-consuming and expensive to operate (use of technology helps reduce these).

If the "arguments for" win in your organisation, you have to decide which method to adopt. The main methods of formal job evaluation and their advantages and disadvantages are summarised[2] in Figure 5.3.

> **Benchmark jobs**
> These are jobs that are well known in the organisation, clearly defined, representative of levels and functions and, ideally, the relativities between them will be well established. They should be jobs which can be matched with jobs outside the organisation for market rate survey purposes.

If the "arguments against" win in your organisation, then "informal job evaluation" will be the order of the day. This happens in lots of organisations, large and small, which have a well-established hierarchy of roles that are already clearly defined in terms of factors such as, experience, reporting relationship, people management or competency level. These organisations, maybe like yours, see little advantage in

FIGURE 5.3   Comparison of job evaluation methods

Method	Brief description	Advantages	Disadvantages
Job ranking	Job are compared with one another and placed in rank order.	Simple and quick to use.	No defined standards. Not acceptable in equal value cases.
Paired comparison	Whole jobs are ranked by the statistical method of paired comparison.	Easier to compare two jobs at one time than having to make multi-comparisons.	No defined standards. Not acceptable in equal value cases.
Job classification	The characteristics of the grades in a structure are defined and jobs are slotted.	Quick and easy to use. Definitions guide grading decisions.	Can't cope with complex jobs. Not acceptable in equal value cases.
Factor comparison	Benchmark jobs are evaluated against common factors and the score is converted directly into monetary terms. Remaining jobs are slotted into pay bands by reference to benchmark jobs.	Analytical. No need for definitions of job levels. Directly prices jobs.	Depends on "right" benchmark jobs. Complex. Subjective judgement still required.
Point-factor rating	Jobs are assessed in terms of the degree to which defined factors are present; points are allocated for each factor according to the level at which this factor is present in the job; the points for each factor are combined to give a total score.	Definitions guide grading decisions. Credible – probably be perceived as fair and objective.	Complex. Spurious impression of scientific accuracy. Judgement still required.
Competence-related evaluation (factor-based)	Competencies used as factor headings as in a points factor scheme.	As for point-factor rating. Additionally, directs attention to people and their roles. Could be integrated with competence framework.	As for point-factor; additionally: Judgement needed. Depends on robust competence analysis. Competence profiles don't necessarily translate readily into evaluation factors. Danger of paying for acquisition of competencies rather than their use.

introducing a formal job evaluation process which, in their eyes, will just confirm what exists already and many of them don't like the administration involved. However, some organisations do use role or level descriptions to allocate employees to appropriate roles and, of course, this has pay implications. In addition, the descriptions make like-for-like comparisons when benchmarking pay and benefits against the external salary market, that much easier than if they didn't exist.

Job evaluation – formal or informal – should, quite simply, help overcome difficulties in managing internal relativities and maintaining competitive pay levels. The decision about how you achieve that is yours.

Pay bands and pay progression

The second issue that The Together Company considers when it's selecting an appropriate pay framework is "pay bands and pay progression".

Progression without pay bands

When spot rates are used (the base pay of everybody in a given job is the same) pay progression can happen in two ways: everybody gets the same annual increase in base pay and there's no opportunity to earn more for performance; or everybody gets the same annual increase in base pay and they are eligible for a performance related bonus which isn't consolidated into base pay.

Progression within pay bands

When pay bands are used these can apply to individual jobs or a range of different jobs grouped into grades as a result of formal job evaluation, for example. In both cases pay bands are usually defined around the market reference point – typically the market median salary – which is determined by carrying out market research into the pay at other organisations (Chapter 6, Understanding your employment market: pay and benefits).

In The Together Company pay bands provide the opportunity to link pay increases to a wide range of factors, such as performance, skill, competence and knowledge, or a combination of these. The band width depends simply on the extent to which the organisation wants to do this – the greater the scope the greater the width – and the rate of pay progression within the band. Band width usually varies with job size too:

at the lower end of the pay framework a band width of plus and minus 10% of the market reference point is fairly typical; at the top end, 25%. In some organisations, however, differences in performance, skill, competence and knowledge demand much broader pay bands, for example, the band maximum is twice or three times the band minimum. This is usually called a "broad band".

Pay bands are typically divided into "zones" which reflect the level of "contribution" or "worth" in terms of performance, skill or competence. Figure 5.4 is an example of a performance-zoned pay band.

FIGURE 5.4   Performance-zoned pay band

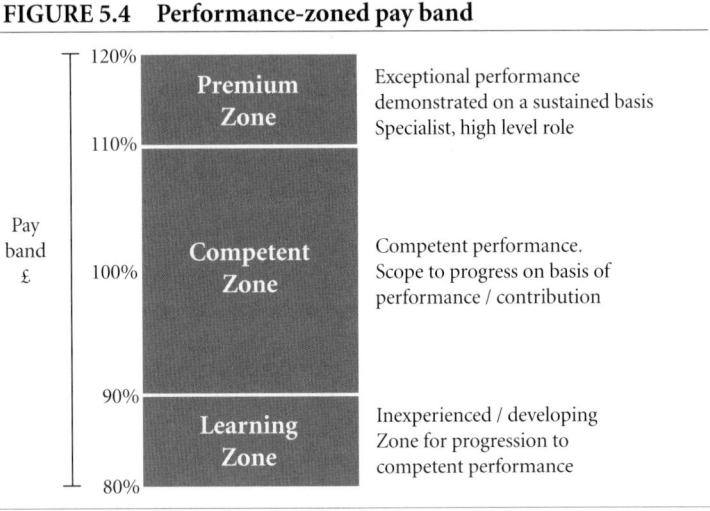

It defines three stages through which individuals might go, starting at the bottom of the pay band. These are:

- **Learning zone:** someone with the basic qualifications for the job but lacks the necessary experience to perform at the competent level would start in this zone. The zone is defined from 80-90% but it could be varied according to the average length of learning for the job in your organisation.
- **Competent zone:** this represents the range of pay for competent performers. The 100% point in the band is the market reference point, for example the market median. Scope is provided for employees to advance above 100% on the basis of their performance.
- **Premium zone:** this zone is reserved for employees whose performance is exceptional – and it is sustained at that level – or a long-term increase in their responsibilities justifies pay at this level. Care must be taken to ensure that employees don't drift into this zone.

There are two other important design points about pay bands in The Together Company:

- They often overlap to acknowledge that an experienced employee performing well can be of more value to your organisation than a new employee in the grade above
- Differentials between pay bands are large enough to reflect increases in job size. Not less than 10% at the lower end of the framework and around 20% at the upper end (excluding top management) is fairly typical. For broad pay bands and for management roles, differentials of 25% to 50% might be required.

In most organisations pay progression is decided at the annual pay review when managers are issued with guidelines for deciding appropriate increases. David Lloyd Leisure uses a pay matrix which takes into account an employee's performance and where their salary sits in the pay band for their job. A Team Member rated Outstanding, but paid below the middle, for example, will receive a higher increase than someone rated Growing, but paid above the middle. Illustrative increases are shown in Figure 5.5, where "X" is the percentage increase an Achieving employee paid at the middle of the scale, would receive.

FIGURE 5.5 Pay Review Matrix – Illustrative example at David Lloyd Leisure			
Performance Rating	*Base*	*Middle*	*Upper*
Unacceptable	0	0	0
Growing	X minus 33%	X minus 33%	X minus 66%
Achieving	X plus 33%	X	X minus 33%
Exceeding	X plus 66%	X plus 33%	X
Outstanding	2X	X plus 66%	X plus 33%

Resolving the three pay framework problems

Three common problems account for most of the reasons pay frameworks lose credibility. Here are some practical tips for resolving them.

Problem 1: Too many employees at the top of their pay band

This can have serious cost consequences and occurs for three reasons:

- Managers allow employees to drift to the top of the pay band irrespective of their performance

- The whole pay band comprises incremental steps that relate to years in the job, so when an employee reaches the top, there's no further increase in base pay
- Market rates have increased, but pay bands haven't been updated sufficiently.

Actions to resolve this include:

- Re-communicate your pay policy to everybody – this is a "must-do"
- Define the percentage of employees you expect to be rated in each performance category – for every department and stick to it. Variations should be agreed only in exceptional circumstances and supported by concrete evidence
- Freeze base salary and pay non-consolidated performance bonuses to those who deserve them
- Obtain market data on benchmark jobs in the pay band and increase the band accordingly
- Stop incremental steps at their current level and create a "performance-pay zone" at the top end of an existing pay band. The width of this band could increase each year to provide increasingly greater scope to reward performance and keep a check on base pay costs.

Problem 2: High performers on relatively low pay

The most serious potential consequence of this is best performers leave. The high performer on relatively low pay scenario arises for two reasons. First, the employee's starting salary, on joining the organisation or being promoted, is low compared to other employees doing the same job. Second, pay progression has not reflected their performance because monitoring of pay awards and the performance distribution has been lax or non-existent. Actions to rectify this situation include:

- Introduce a pay review matrix that takes into account position in pay band and performance. That way, "higher performers" receive a bigger slice of the annual pay increase pot
- Introduce a six-monthly pay review for the most anomalous cases, so the "pay-gap" is reduced more quickly
- A one-time ad-hoc programme of adjustments to base pay.

Problem 3: Conflict between market rates and job evaluation results

This arises when market data suggests that a job should be in one pay band and job evaluation says it should be in a different one. This manifests itself in two ways. First, when specific skills and knowledge are in short supply, so market pay for employees in these roles is significantly higher than that determined through benchmarking at the time of job evaluation. To increase the pay band on the basis of those jobs alone would raise (perhaps unjustifiably) the base pay of everybody else in that band, irrespective of the job they do. Second, when there's been an over-supply of specific skills, so market rates have fallen and employees end up being "overpaid". However, it's usually impossible (unless agreed contractually) and potentially unfair to employees in other roles in the band, for whom pay is "market competitive", to reduce the band. But if you take no action, some employees (who could be the best performers) may leave because they know they're underpaid and can get a better package in a competitor, and other employees (who could be the worst performers) stay because they know they're overpaid.

Potential solutions to this problem include:

- Replace a one-size-fits-all set of pay bands by job family based pay bands which are linked directly to market rates
- Introduce broad banding – market benchmarked rigorously
- Introduce pay supplements based on clearly defined criteria, such as geographic region (experiencing recruitment difficulties) or specific skill sets
- Red-circle jobs for which market rates have fallen and progressively reduce the level of annual pay increase until these jobs have been brought into line with market rates. You need to make sure that what you do is legally sound, of course.

Is it right for you?

The pay framework that's right for your organisation will depend on your particular needs. Examples of choices that might be made according to circumstances are set out below.

Small but growing organisation

You operate in a highly competitive market and are not over-concerned with equal-value considerations. The simplest approach would be to define each job clearly and use market data (Chapter 6, Understanding your employment market: pay and benefits) to determine a spot rate. This would allow you to reward performance through bonus. Alternatively, you might start by ranking key and easily recognisable jobs, such as receptionist, team leader, IT specialist and accountant, and place them in broadly-defined job levels which you "price" by reference to market data. Spot rates and performance bonuses would work here too. On the other hand, a salary range for each job level would allow performance and / or competence-related pay progression through the band.

You could easily undertake the job level exercise and obtain market without any specialist help from outside advisors. It would not protect you from equal-value claims, but involving employees in the job level exercise would help to ensure the framework was perceived to be fair.

Fairly large organisation

Your organisation is structured on a well-defined hierarchical basis. You are keen to avoid gender bias, not just evade an equal-value case. You might develop a point-factor job evaluation scheme taking particular care to avoid discrimination in the selection of factors and any weighting. You would evaluate benchmark jobs, define grades, allocate benchmark jobs and slot all remaining jobs into the framework. The final step would be to obtain market data for the benchmark jobs and develop pay bands for each grade. You would want to involve employees and, if you have trades unions or consultative committees, their representatives. Unless your HR department has specialist knowledge of job evaluation, competence analysis and pay frameworks, you may want to obtain advice from consultants.

Project-team based organisation

Your organisation is based around projects and teams, with a strong emphasis on people and key roles. A flexible pay framework is crucial, especially if formal job evaluation is to be involved, so you would probably want to base the framework on competence and generic roles. An existing competency framework, which you use for employee selection and development, for example, coupled with broad pay bands, could be ideal. This would allow you to position people in the bands in accordance with their level of competence, performance and the market rate for their role. If you don't have a competence framework, forming a working group (which could include consultants) to develop one would be the starting point.

High-tech / professional services organisation

Your organisation is structured into teams of knowledge workers and service functions such as finance, HR and marketing, who work closely with manufacturing or client-facing teams. You might decide to adopt a job family approach using competence definitions to identify levels of contribution and market pricing to determine salaries. An existing competency framework would give you a head-start otherwise you would need to develop one. If you have some form of formal job evaluation, for example point-factor rating, you might want to retain it in order to achieve internal equity between job families. Alternatively, if you don't use formal job evaluation, you could use competence levels and market pricing to determine relativities within job families and carry out some form of factor comparison only where you believe there is a need to establish comparative worth.

Key points

- A pay framework is not optional – your organisation needs to communicate the basis for paying people.
- A pay framework should fit your organisation – its culture and market place – and there's always plenty of choice.
- Your aim should be a pay framework that mirrors employees' perceptions of different jobs and levels and what they and you perceive to be important in terms of pay progression.
- Job evaluation – formal or informal – is a process for determining the relative worth of jobs in an organisation and, because pay has to be managed internally and maintained competitively, no organisation can avoid it. The decision about how you achieve that is yours.
- Managers and employees who are well trained and educated in the purpose of a pay framework will go a long way to satisfying the twin demands for fairness and market competitiveness.
- Monitor how the pay framework is working in relation to what was expected – do the highest performers receive the highest rewards, is competence increasing and how do employees feel about its fairness?

CHAPTER SIX

Understanding your employment market: pay and benefits

At a glance

Lots of organisations are "obsessed with pay", just like insurance companies who advertise on television are with price. But, if your organisation is to stand any chance of attracting and retaining the right people, offering market-competitive pay alone isn't enough. While getting the pay part of the package right is a "must-do" for all organisations, employee benefits and work-life practices are increasing competitive differentiators. Without a comprehensive and competitive package, it won't be long before some of your employees start to look elsewhere for work and prospective employees realise that your organisation is not the place for them. This is why The Together Company knows its employment market inside out.

Before I explore how The Together Company goes about understanding the employment market and getting the data it needs to offer a competitive package, I'll say what I mean by "competitive". For a software company facing severe recruitment pressures for skills in short supply, this might mean paying base salaries in the upper quartile market range across the UK's IT sector and providing flexible benefits (Chapter 12, Customised reward strategies). For a manufacturing company in an area of high unemployment, paying around the market median in the local marketplace and providing a fixed package of benefits, might be sufficient to recruit the people it needs.

For many jobs, pay is sector specific, such as financial services or pharmaceuticals and benefits are not, so it's important to be clear about your employment market and where your organisation wants to position itself in relation to the competition. In fact, who is the competition? One more thing: good quality market data about pay, benefits and other rewards doesn't have to cost a fortune; it's a sound investment in attracting and retaining talented people.

Five steps to understanding your employment market

By following five key steps you can obtain reliable, accurate and up-to-date information about market rates and trends, which enables you to make informed decisions about the content and value of the reward package your organisation provides to employees.

Step 1: Knowing what you must provide by law

There are minimum levels of benefits and terms of employment that the law requires of companies operating in the UK. While, for many organisations, these may not be sufficient to attract and retain talented people, they are a useful benchmark reference point which The Together Company never loses sight of. The main requirements[1] including those introduced under the Work & Families Act 2006[2,3], are summarised below:

National Minimum Wage: Employers must meet the requirements of the legislation.

Annual leave: All employees are entitled to a minimum of 20 days paid annual holiday.

Pensions: All organisations employing five or more people have to offer access to an approved stakeholder pension scheme. Essentially, these are low cost personal pensions regulated by the government and provided through pension companies. So, for the majority of employers, the decision is not whether to offer access to a pension scheme, but whether to contribute to one and, if so, which type. The decision will reflect the organisation's overall benefits strategy that is aligned to organisational objectives.

Working time: The working week is capped at 48 hours, averaged over 17 weeks, for employees who have not 'opted out', although it is often around 37 to 40 hours. The Working Time Regulations also provide for minimum rest periods and make special provision for night work.

Parental leave: There is a right to 13 weeks unpaid parental leave for men and women at any time up to the child's fifth birthday. This must be taken in blocks or multiples of one week, with 21 days notice given to the employer.

Time off for dependant care: The right to take unpaid time off to deal with family emergencies (eg concerning an elderly parent, partner, child or other person living as part of the family).

Maternity & adoption leave: Women giving birth are entitled to 39 weeks maternity leave. Employees who qualify are entitled to an extra 13 weeks additional maternity leave, making 52 weeks in total. It is unlawful to dismiss anyone on the grounds of pregnancy and childbirth, and contracts of employment continue during all periods of statutory maternity and adoption leave.

Paternity leave: Fathers are entitled to 2 weeks paid paternity leave, which can be taken as a single block of one or two weeks within the 56 days following the child's birth. In the second 6 months of the child's life, fathers will be entitled to additional paid leave of up to 3 months and further unpaid leave of up to 3 months. This is dependent on the mother giving up all or part of her maternity leave after her first 6 months and returning to work.

Right to request flexible working: Employees with children under 6 (under 18 if disabled) and carers of adults can request a change in their hours, time or place of work. The employer can refuse such a request on specified business grounds but must follow a detailed procedure.

Part-time work: Part-timers are entitled to the same hourly rate of pay and the same entitlements to annual leave and maternity/parental leave on a pro rata basis as full-timers. Part-timers must also have the same entitlement to contractual sick pay and no less favourable treatment in access to training.

One final point. Always check the legislation and the details of the above provisions: entitlements, for example, to the above provisions usually depend on the employee having no less than a defined number of weeks continues service.

Step 2: Defining the competition

Who does your organisation compete with for people? Where are they located – locally, regionally, nationally – perhaps internationally for some business leaders? Comparisons in mainstream sectors, such as financial services or retail, are easy because there's usually a clear reference set of similar organisations. But, outside the mainstream, comparisons can be difficult because different job roles can't be pigeon-holed and the sector's either too small or too specialised to get market information. Whenever possible, agreeing a list of reference organisations is desirable – and once you've got that list, keep to it. Organisations come and go of course, so you need to update the list, but if you change most of it each year you stand little chance of measuring, on a consistent basis, what's happening to market pay and benefits. In fact, the odds that pay levels have increased or decreased are probably equal – although suggesting that market pay has gone down can be a difficult argument to defend, even in a low inflation economy.

There's one more point here: the "market The Together Company competes in" for talent is still just one; however, it may be more difficult to have benchmarking data on benefits for its chosen competitors / sectors, so more generic market data may be needed.

Step 3: Deciding how to get market information

The Together Company researches its employment market for two broad categories of information:

Pay: base salary and variable pay, such as incentives, bonus, commission, profit share payments and shift or overtime premium; and
Benefits: such as holidays, pensions, healthcare, company cars, mortgage assistance, sick pay, relocation packages and insurances (travel, dental, life, personal accident).

There are four main sources of information:

- Published and participant-only based surveys
- Websites / job advertisements
- Salary and benefits survey clubs; and
- Personal contacts.

Figure 6.1 summarises the key features of each and their advantages and disadvantages.

Costs of market information vary widely – definitely a case of "you get what you pay for." You won't get much from a published survey costing £100 – probably base salary for a handful of "generic job titles" and some very general data about incentives and benefits. £500, however, will usually buy information about base salary, bonus, commission and profit share payments, for a specific function such as accounting, marketing or information technology. If you need market data about several functions check that the jobs covered by the survey are a fairly good match with the ones in your organisation, otherwise you won't get value for money.

These "off-the-shelf" published surveys may give some information about employee benefits, but if you want comprehensive market data about a wide range of benefits, buying a specialist employee benefits survey is by far the best option.

£2,000 will usually enable you to take part in a participant-only based survey run (by

FIGURE 6.1   Sources of market data

Source	Features	Advantages	Disadvantages
Published and participant-only based surveys	Most published surveys give base salary and bonus information, often by geographic region and industrial sector, but if you want benefits information, you'll need to look at specialist surveys. Participant-only based surveys which companies subscribe to, usually annually, oftern provide a wide range of pay and benefits information	Wide coverage, readily available. Specialist surveys deal with particular job groups in depth. Participant-only based surveys usually achieve good job matching	Published surveys run the risk of imprecise job matching, although some, (including participant-only based surveys) give job matching criteria. The gap between data collection and publication means data is not "up-to-the minute". Can be expensive.
Websites / job advertisements	Some websites enable users to input their own salary data into a confidential database and receive a market report. Others provide salaries for job vacancies in different sectors or parts of the UK. The recruitment columns of national or local newspapers and trade or professional journals give salary data.	Readily available, highly visible indications of market rates and trends, up-to-date.	Job matching is very imprecise and salary data can be misleading – it's not always what's paid. Organisations will pay more for highly experienced candidates and less for those who don't quite match the job specification.
Salary and benefits survey clubs	Groups of companies, usually in the same sector, which exchange market data, confidentiality. Often run by consultants, for the club. Clubs usually meet once or twice a year, following survey results, to discuss the findings and exchange experience.	Reasonably precise job and company matching. Can provide lots of detail on pay structures and benefits. Opportunity to forge good relationships with other organisations.	Sample size may be too small, relies on goodwill of participants to conduct survey.
Personal contacts	Talking to personal contacts in other organisations helps build up a picture of "what's going on in the market place" for example, recruitment pressures, sign-on bonuses and new approaches to reward that might be of benefit to your organisation.	Valuable insights about company reward policy, annual increases. Specialist recruitment agencies often have a good "feel" for salaries, bonuses and employee benefits.	Can be imprecise on detail.

a consultancy for example) for your sector. You'll need to provide data about your jobs and you'll receive a comprehensive report in return. Many such survey providers offer bespoke analyses too, such as basic salary for a group of chosen competitors or additional benefits information. Bespoke analyses are, of course, at an additional cost.

Market data on recruitment websites tends to be free. Alternatively, you can pay a specialist survey provider to carry out a market survey or subscribe to one of their regular participant-only based surveys. Fees depend on the number of jobs and the range of data and analysis you require. This goes for salary and benefits survey clubs too.

The cost of salary and benefits survey clubs depends on the scale and scope. In some clubs a few companies are sponsors; they drive the survey and give more financial backing than other participants. In other clubs every participant pays the same subscription fee.

Unless you take part in a salary and benefits survey club which provides all the market data you need, more than one source of information should be used (if time and finances permit of course) Three is ideal. This is for two reasons:

- It gives a balanced view of the market place and no survey can be designed to show that one salary level is the "correct market rate" for any given job
- One source is unlikely to provide all the information you need.

When you have several sources to choose from, focus on those that provide information for benchmark jobs which should typically cover around 70-80% of employees. The jobs remaining can be compared to the benchmark jobs and notional market rates determined.

Step 4: Comparing like with like

Comparisons on the basis of job title alone are risky. They might be fine for jobs that are fairly well prescribed such as receptionists (unless they are bilingual, for example) or graduate trainees, but not for most other jobs. The Together Company makes comparisons on the basis of job responsibilities and the size of its business, typically measured by number of employees and sales. Pay levels usually vary by geographic region, such as South West or North East, so it makes sure that published surveys, for example, have the appropriate regionally based information.

There's another important point about using published surveys and that's sample sizes. This covers the number of companies reporting data for each job and the number of job holders reported. These can vary widely: many large published surveys report data on hundreds of employees. When this isn't the case, look for a minimum of six companies reporting data for each job and at least ten job holders per job.

Data on jobs in fast-moving industries, such as information technology and media, becomes quickly out-of-date. Look for data that's no more than 12 months old. To ensure you stay ahead of the market or at least don't lag behind, it's usually advisable to look at earnings forecasts for the next 12 months.

Step 5: Exercising judgment when interpreting market data

The translation of market data into competitive pay and benefits levels is a process based on judgment and compromise. It involves striking a reasonable balance between the merits of the different data sources used. This is an intuitive process.

In relation to pay, people often refer to "the market rate", but there is no such thing as a definitive market rate for any job, even when comparing identically sized organisations in the same sector and location. Different surveys of the same types of jobs produce different results because the sample size, job matching, timing and participating companies all vary. However, that doesn't stop some top executives and HR people who are not familiar with the problems of carrying out market comparisons, believing that it's possible to find out exactly the market rate for any job, at a given age and experience or skill level, in any location or sector, to the nearest pound or euro! Individuals as well as jobs have market rates, so when The Together Company interprets market information, it decides the rate for the job and the rate for the person in the job – that will be influenced by their experience and performance.

In relation to benefits, comparisons are not as straightforward as pay. Benefits packages vary widely in levels of provision, eligibility, restrictions in relation to some healthcare benefits, for example and whether employees are required to contribute financially to any specific benefits. While the costs of providing benefits may be known in most organisations, the financial value to employees is known in far fewer. Even when it is, costs and value can hide the myriad of variations mentioned above.

Guidance for assessing both pay and benefits in relation to the competition is given next.

Assessing pay competitiveness

One of the analyses we at Strategic Reward do for clients is to calculate a "competitive index" for each job surveyed. This compares the organisation's actual base salary and the market reference point, for example the market median (Figure 6.2). The competitive index of 101.8 for Administrator says the organisation pays 1.8% above the market median while the competitive index of 89.5 for Receptionist says the organisation pays 89.5% of the market median or 11.5% below the market median. However, the competitive index doesn't imply that the salaries paid by the organisation are "over-competitive" or "under-competitive". An organisation may, for example, value some jobs more highly or lowly than the competition, so a gap between what it and the competition pay is expected.

FIGURE 6.2   Pay: Comparing your organisation and the market

Job	LQ	Median	UQ	Average	Company Actual	Competitive Index
Secretary	12,450	14,750	17,450	14,450	13,995	94.9
Receptionist	11,250	13,345	16,250	12,250	11,950	89.5
Administrator	11,350	13,115	15,350	12,350	13,350	101.8
Sales Advisor	13,450	16,230	18,450	15,450	17,600	108.4

Faced with such a range of competitive indices, how might you apply your annual salary increase budget to produce an equitable outcome? I recently helped an engineering company resolve this issue by developing a scale of salary increases which brought the range reference points for all jobs within an acceptable competitive index range of 97.5 to 102.49 (Figure 6.3).

FIGURE 6.3   Applying market data to pay band reference points

Competitive index of...	Increase in reference point
107.50 to 112.49	0%
102.50 to 107.49	1.5%
97.50 to 102.49	3.5%
92.50 to 97.49	5.5%
87.50 to 92.49	7.5%

Assessing benefits competitiveness

The most practical approach is to compare the key features of each benefit. Figure 6.4 sets out criteria for doing so.

FIGURE 6.4   Benefits: Comparing your organisation and the market

Employee benefit	Assessment criteria
Holiday entitlement	Number of days on joining; days at defined years of service
Pensions	Accrual rate in a final salary scheme Employee contribution rate and employer contribution rate in both defined benefit (final salary) and defined contribution (money purchase) plans Death-in-service benefit Value of dependents pensions
Life assurance	Multiple of salary
Private healthcare insurance	Cost to employer Cost to employee Excess paid
Permanent health insurance	Cost to employee Number of weeks before benefit is paid
Sick pay	Number of weeks at full pay Number of weeks at reduced pay and level of reduction
Company cars / cash alternative	Lease cost or purchase price Cash alternative per job level Petrol provision (free or cost) Specific items included for example, servicing
Leisure / social benefits	Budget per employee for social activities Discount at leisure clubs
Flexible benefits	Range of benefits offered How often employees can make selections Average savings per employee

This type of analysis is invaluable when assessing the viability of introducing more flexible and customised reward strategies (Chapter 12).

Is it right for you?

The market research that's right for your organisation will depend on your particular needs. Examples of choices that might be made according to circumstances are set out below.

Small but growing organisation

Your organisation is small and has limited financial resources for market research into pay and benefits. But it operates in a highly competitive marketplace, so you need to keep track of what the competition is doing. You have a mixture of specialist roles, for example market researchers and well recognised roles, for example administrative assistants.

A practical and low cost approach would be:

- Review recruitment websites (search engine route) and on-line job advertisements in appropriate newspapers (regional or national) and trade journals
- Use personal contacts: these might be business contacts in other organisations or sector associations, people applying for jobs, people leaving – ask them what's being offered
- Talk to recruitment agencies that specialise in your sector or location.

This approach would enable you to monitor the marketplace almost on an on-going basis, without the need to buy several published surveys to cover all your roles.

Fairly large organisation

Your organisation is structured along fairly traditional lines – business divisions and central support functions. You have lots of people doing well recognised roles, such as administrative assistant and customer service advisor, and a few people doing a wide range of specialist roles in marketing, research and development and information technology.

The ideal approach would be to join a salary and benefits club for your sector. You might be able to join an existing club run by one of your competitors or a third party, for example a HR consultancy. While it's not the cheapest approach (costs vary enormously) the club would give you opportunity to meet fellow participating organisations and to discuss the results and reward trends in your sector. Alternatively, you could take part in a participant-only salary run by a third party. In addition to receiving the standard survey report – usually annually, but in fast-moving sectors such as IT / telecommunications and media, probably twice a year –

you might be to request bespoke analyses about specific jobs or companies.

Both approaches should offer high quality information based on good job matching.

High tech or professional services organisation

Your organisation employs people to do mainly specialised roles such as legal, professional engineering and consulting, research and development, pharmaceuticals or information technology, with traditional support services such as finance, marketing and HR. A two pronged approach will be needed:

- For specialist roles: join a salary survey club or a participant-only based salary and (ideally) benefits survey for specialist roles. The advantages (Figure 6.1) will far outweigh the costs.

- For well-recognised roles (administrative or finance for example):
    - Review recruitment websites (search engine route) and on-line job advertisements in appropriate newspapers (regional or national)
    - Use personal contacts: these might be business contacts in other organisations or sector associations, people applying for jobs, people leaving – ask them what's being offered

Key points

- Make sure you satisfy the legal requirements for pay, benefits and work-life practices.
- Decide who your organisation competes with for talent – chosen competitors / sectors – and that might vary by type of job.
- Compare like with like, in terms of job responsibilities and size, geographic locations and industrial sectors. Never compare solely on job title.
- Obtain accurate and representative data on market rates and what the competition provides. If the data is a few months old, update it on a pro-rata basis, using published data on annual pay increases.
- Don't rely on one source of information – try to obtain some background data and use personal contacts. In terms of data quality, you get what you pay for.
- Individuals as well as jobs have market rates –so take this into account when setting pay.
- Translating market data into competitive rewards for individuals requires judgment and compromise. Educate managers and employees about how you do it.
- Don't just copy the competition – think about how you can differentiate your pay, benefits and work-life practices from the competition, to give a competitive edge.

CHAPTER SEVEN
Equal pay

At a glance

The Together Company is committed firmly to the principle of equal pay and meeting the requirements of The Equal Pay Act. But it doesn't take "equality" to mean that everybody is treated in the same way. The key here is "fairness".

Do you know whether your organisation's pay practices provide for equal pay? Do they reward men and women equally? If not, your organisation could be challenged under the Equal Pay Act 1970, which gives women (or men) a right to equal pay for equal work. An employer can only pay a man more than a women for doing equal work if there is a genuine and material reason for doing so which is not related to sex. This chapter gives an overview of what's involved[1].

A simple speedy check

A simple speedy check to establish whether your organisation is an equal pay employer is set out below:

1. Does your organisation have a stated policy on equal pay?
2. Has the equal pay policy been communicated to employees and recognised representatives, for example trade unions?
3. Has responsibility for the implementation of the policy been clearly assigned?
4. Have you carried out an equal pay review comparing the pay of men and women doing equal work, in line with the Equal Opportunities Commission's (EOC) Code of Practice?
5. Does your organisation use a single job evaluation scheme covering all employees that has been designed and implemented so as not to discriminate on grounds of sex?

If you answer "Yes" to all questions your organisation has taken the key steps to begin to address the question of equal pay. You should continue regularly to review all aspects of your pay framework (Chapter 5, A pay framework) and reward practices.

If you answer "No" to questions 4 and 5, this indicates that you can't be confident your organisation is an equal pay employer. An equal pay review will help you to determine whether you have a gender pay gap.

The EOC five-step model

The Together Company uses the five-step equal pay review model recommended by the EOC. This is summarised below:

Step 1: Deciding the scope of the review and identifying the data required
Step 2: Determining where men and women are doing equal work
Step 3: Collecting and comparing pay data to identify any significant equal pay gaps
Step 4: Establishing the causes of any significant pay gaps and deciding whether these are free from discrimination
Step 5: Developing an equal pay action plan and / or reviewing and monitoring.

Even if you decide to use an independent consultancy to help carry out an equal pay review, rather than carry out the review using entirely in-house resources, make sure you fully understand what's involved. You, not the consultancy, will be responsible for acting on the results. The EOC provides lots of information and guidance about following this five-step process. This covers areas such as:

- The legal framework
- Data required for pay reviews
- Statistical analyses
- Job evaluation schemes free of sex bias
- Assessing equal value, and
- Reviewing your payments systems, policies and practices.

Aspects covered by Equal Pay

The Equal Pay Act covers far more than "pay". All aspects of the pay and benefits package are covered, including those below:

- Basic pay
- Non-discretionary bonuses
- Overtime rates
- Allowances
- Access to pensions schemes
- Benefits under pension schemes
- Hours of work
- Company cars and allowances

- Performance related benefits
- Redundancy pay and benefits
- Sick pay
- Other benefits, for example travel allowances

These aspects have implications for other key areas of reward policy such as job evaluation, pay on appointment, promotion or transfer, pay progression, monitoring market rates and performance reviews.

Foundation of an equal pay review

Three key checks are the foundation of an equal pay review at The Together Company:

Check 1: Like work

Is where men and women are doing work which is the same or broadly similar. Men and women are likely to be doing like work where they have the same job title, or where, even if their job titles differ, they do the same or broadly similar work.

Check 2: Work rated as equivalent

Is where men and women have had their jobs rated as equivalent under an analytical job evaluation scheme (Chapter 5, A pay framework). Men and women are likely to be doing work rated as equivalent where they have similar, not necessarily the same, job evaluation scores and are in the same grade.

Check 3: Equal value

Work of equal value is work that is different but which is of equal value in terms of the demands of the job. "Demands" mean the knowledge, skills, physical and mental effort and responsibilities that the job requires.

If any of the three checks reveal either:

- Significant differences (5% of more) between the basic pay or total earnings of men and women performing equal work, or
- Patterns of basic pay difference (3% or more), for example, women consistently earning less than men for equal work at most, or all, grades or levels in the organisation,

further investigation is needed. If there is no satisfactory explanation for gaps between men's and women's pay, you need to implement an equal pay action plan. This might include the development of an equal pay policy.

If an equal pay review reveals no gaps between men's and women's pay, you need to review and monitor practices to ensure they stay that way

Equal pay policy – a model example

The Together Company has an equal pay policy which reflects EOC guidelines. These are modified in accordance with any discussions with, and commitments made by The Together Company to employee's representatives. A model example is shown below:

"We are committed to the principle of equal pay for all our employees. We aim to eliminate any sex bias in our pay practices.

We understand that equal pay between men and women is a legal right under both domestic and European law.

It is in the interest of our organisation to ensure that we have fair and just pay practices. It is important that employees have confidence in the process of eliminating sex bias and we are therefore committed to working in partnership with employee's representatives. As good business practice we are committed to working with employee's representatives to take action to ensure we provide equal pay.

We believe that in eliminating sex bias in our pay practices we are sending a positive message to our employees and customers. It makes good business sense to have fair and transparent reward practices and it helps us to control costs. We recognise that avoiding unfair discrimination will improve morale and enhance efficiency.

Our objectives are to:

- Eliminate any unfair, unjust or unlawful practices that impact on pay
- Take appropriate remedial action

We will:

- Implement an equal pay review in line with Equal Opportunities Commission (EOC) guidance for all current employees and starting pay for new employees (including those on maternity leave, career breaks, or non-standard contracts), every two years

- Plan and implement actions in partnership with employee's representatives
- Provide training and guidance for those involved in determining pay
- Inform employees of how these practices work and how their own pay is determined
- Respond to grievances on equal pay as a priority
- In conjunction with employee's representatives, monitor pay statistics annually".

Is it right for you?

Yes! The Equal Pay Act applies to all organisations and whatever kind of equal pay review process is used the essential features are the same for any size of organisation:

- Comparing the pay of men and women doing equal work
- Explaining any equal pay gaps
- Closing those pay gaps that can't satisfactorily be explained on grounds other than sex.

By providing equal pay, The Together Company avoids expensive tribunal claims, protects and strengthens its public image, reduces recruitment costs and demonstrates a genuine commitment to equal opportunities. All help it to attract and retain the best people.

Key points

- Equal pay is not just about "pay". It's about virtually all aspects of the pay and benefits package.
- An equal pay review is not simply a data collection exercise. Employee involvement is important too. Without that the validity of the review and success of subsequent action taken may be questioned.
- Equal pay is a commitment by your organisation to put right any gender pay inequalities, so the review must have the involvement and support of managers with the authority to deliver the necessary changes – that's usually the Board.

Part two
Reward choices

These are the specific reward practices which support (sometimes drive) the four core business objectives of The Together Company. Some of you may be surprised that there are four only. But I believe focus on the few, success-critical objectives is what matters most. Too many objectives leads to the really important ones being lost; that dilutes resources put into achieving them and is confusing for employees (shareholders and customers too).

Rewarding team excellence

Getting people to work together – within the same part of the organisation and between different parts of it – is an elusive goal for many organisations. But unless people put the team's or the organisation's objectives before their own personal agenda, actual business performance will always fall significantly short of what could be achieved. Rewarding team excellence financially and / or non-financially says "teamwork is important here". Tailoring rewards to the type of team and people's motivations are the keys to success.

Rewarding customer satisfaction

Employees working together, of course, should be good for customer satisfaction. Most of us have experience of "the left hand not knowing what the right hand is doing" and it doesn't fill us with confidence that what we have asked for will be done to our satisfaction. By rewarding customer satisfaction the organisation communicates its importance – to employees, customers and shareholders. Dissatisfied customers are bad for profits and that's bad news for pay rises too.

Sharing in financial success

This may not make employees work harder, but I believe it does draw their attention to the organisation's performance and how that affects their pay. That, alone, may encourage employees to try to understand the business and consequently help to make them work smarter in the long term. There is an increasing body of research evidence, for example The Value Profit Chain work by Harvard Business School, which suggests that employee satisfaction, customer satisfaction and financial results are linked.

Rewarding business leaders

The actions of business leaders have a major impact on the fortunes of the organisations they lead. Not only that, how they are rewarded should (but doesn't always) set the tone for rewards throughout the organisation. That means aligning rewards for business leaders and the business objectives of owners. In many publicly-quoted companies business leaders are encouraged (sometimes required) to maintain a substantial personal shareholding in the company, and the size of future rewards often depends on it.

CHAPTER EIGHT

Rewarding team excellence

Case study

Rewarding team spirit at Starbucks

Starbucks Coffee Company recognises a team of partners (employees are called partners) for a single, exceptional achievement that reflects one or more of the six guiding principles of Starbucks Mission Statement. The principles are:

- Provide a great work environment and treat each other with respect and dignity.
- Embrace diversity as an essential component in the way we do business.
- Apply the highest standards of excellence to the purchasing, roasting and fresh delivery of our coffee.
- Develop enthusiastically satisfied customers all of the time.
- Contribute positively to our communities and our environment.
- Recognise that profitability is essential to our future success.

What actions and behaviours have been recognised?

Example: A Team Spirit Award was made to the Republic of Ireland project team in 2005 in recognition of their leadership and commitment which contributed to the successful opening of our first Starbucks store in Dublin. The cross-functional team enabled a successful new market launch, overcoming significant challenges including planning regulations, legislation, currency and logistics.

The team celebrated their award by going out as a team for a fabulous dinner with a cocktail or two at a restaurant of their choice.

What is the award?

- A Team Spirit of Starbucks Award memento for each team member
- £20 per team member for a team celebration

Who nominates teams for the award?

- Any partner may nominate any team of partners

Who presents the award?

- The UK Director of the nominated team makes the presentation
- The partner who nominated the team is invited to the award presentation

Rewarding team excellence
At a glance

I recently listened to a presentation given by Bear Grylls, the youngest Briton in 2000 to ascend Mount Everest, about the difference between ordinary and extra-ordinary. Bear talked about the bond that developed between members of the climbing team and how that bond was central to the success of the expedition. He spoke of the trust, reliability and teamwork among the climbers at all times, especially when the whole team or an individual climber faced a critical, sometimes life-threatening, situation.

Like that successful Everest expedition, teamwork is the characteristic spirit of The Together Company. People instinctively put the organisation's priorities before their personal agenda because they know that superior performance (for the organisation and themselves) will be achieved only by working together. While there's collective responsibility for team objectives, each team member also knows what's expected of them individually and they know what everybody else in the team is expected to achieve individually. So, helping and supporting colleagues to raise performance of the whole team comes naturally. When problems arise each person feels comfortable expressing a different point of view if it's for benefit of the team's success.

While most organisations say that teamwork is important, few reward or recognise it. In fact, the reward landscape is covered with examples of individual performance related pay schemes when the organisation wants teamwork. This is where The Together Company differs markedly. It rewards, recognises and celebrates team excellence, regularly and in a wide variety of ways – financial and non-financial.

Four steps to rewarding team excellence

By following four key steps, you too can introduce rewards which help create and reinforce over time, a team-based culture where employees put their team's agenda before their own.

Step 1: Having the support of business leaders

Rewarding team excellence in The Together Company has the unqualified support of business leaders and that starts at the leadership level. They:

- Believe that good teamwork makes a significant contribution to business success
- Agree that superior team performance deserves to be rewarded; and
- Are prepared to give teams scope to manage themselves, if not entirely, at least to a reasonable extent.

Without such support, rewarding team excellence will fail. How does your organisation measure up to the following questions:

- Where does the leadership team stand on the three points above?
- To what extent are people willing to work with each other and put team needs above their own?
- Could reward help achieve team objectives?

If your organisation has only recently moved to a team based way of working, for example, you might feel that to reward team excellence, especially financially, at this stage, would jeopardise some of your broader objectives for developing self-managed teams. However, that shouldn't preclude you from recognising great teamwork in non-financial ways. Alternatively, if lack of teamwork is such a burning issue, this might be the perfect time to bring the issue to the attention of employees by introducing a scheme for rewarding team excellence from the next financial quarter.

Step 2: Deciding where team excellence matters most

Having gained the support of business leaders you will have a clear idea of what you want to achieve by rewarding team excellence and where it's going to be introduced. You might for example, focus on part of your organisation and pilot a scheme for work teams only. Alternatively, you could decide to introduce a scheme for project teams across the whole organisation and review the results in six months to find out where the scheme worked best and why.

The Together Company targets team reward where team excellence matters most. For your organisation, of course, this is something only you can decide by looking at the nature of teams and teamwork – actual or desired. To help you do this, I've grouped all the different types of teams[1] into the three types most commonly found in organisations: work, project and ad hoc teams (sometimes called taskforces). Figure 8.1 gives the key features of each and some examples.

FIGURE 8.1   Types of team in The Together Company

Team	Features	Examples
Work	Permanent part of the organisation Common purpose Members' work is interdependent and they usually control how tasks are performed but not what tasks they do Members may rotate their work, so they become multi-skilled	Insurance claims processing Helpline in a customer contact centre Service team in a car dealership Customer advisor team in a retail bank Production assembly in manufacturing Front of house in a hotel Software development
Project	Set up to complete a specific task Disband after project completion Usually consist of people who have been selected for their skill, knowledge and personal attributes Often have broad mandates Expected to innovate	Product development New-factory or office design and build HR information system development Motorway junction construction Rail franchise bid
Ad hoc	Relatively short-lived – for example, six weeks to six months Formed to solve specific problems and follow a clearly defined process Meet regularly, for example weekly Members continue to perform their regular role in the organisation	Quality improvement Employee survey feedback Energy saving

The tasks and expectations of each type of team differ, so if reward is to have a motivational impact on people in the team, it must be tailored to what they do and what motivates them to give their best.

Step 3: Selecting performance measures

Irrespective of the type of team, The Together Company selects performance measures on the basis of the answer to one key question: "How will team success be defined?" Some guidelines to help you select appropriate performance measures for your organisation are set out below.

Work teams

Performance measures should be derived from organisation objectives. In organisations with very flat structures, say three levels / tiers, where teams are the lowest level, it should be relatively easy to translate the organisation's business objectives directly into team performance measures. However, in multi-tiered structures, organisation objectives must be cascaded through business units and departments and this is when the "line-of-sight" from organisation to work team objectives can become blurred – that is, employees don't understand the connection between the two. The SMART approach discussed in Chapter 3, Performance management can help create objectives that team members really understand and believe in – objectives they know are linked to business success.

You also have to decide if performance measures should be weighted. If you're going to do so, make the weightings meaningful such as 25% or 50%, otherwise employees may consider measures with a low weighting are of low importance. The impact on financial reward in particular will be limited too, unless of course, you have 7 to 10 equally weighted measures, in which case "everything counts!" But this doesn't meet my tests of "simplicity and focus". A few key performance themes should always be your aim.

Project teams

The very different mandates of project teams in organisations means that there isn't a readily available set of generic performance measures on which they can be universally judged. However, the five performance categories below are a good starting point for selecting performance measures across most project teams:

- Quality – adherence to specification or standards
- Customer satisfaction – customer reaction (internal or external) versus expectations
- Cost – actual versus budgeted
- Time – completion date versus scheduled date
- Complexity – such as special technical challenges, multiple working relationships which may involve conflict resolution, degree of innovation and resource restrictions.

All categories may not be appropriate for all projects, of course, so select the ones that are most appropriate for the specific project you have in mind. If complexity is one of the categories, the "sponsors" of the project must agree how complex it is – high, moderate or low, for example. My comments about weighting performance measures for work teams apply to project teams too. If you do need measures in each of the five categories above, the simplest approach is to weight equally. For projects lasting two or three years, for example, it's important to establish performance milestones along the way, perhaps every quarter and assess progress.

Ad hoc teams

As far as ad hoc teams are concerned, performance measures are usually defined as "terms of reference". This is often done to encourage the team to explore and evaluate all potential solutions, rather than quickly adopt a solution that some people in the team have seen work elsewhere. Three brief examples of terms of reference and how success will be measured are given below:

- To improve the process for handling house insurance claims from customers. Team success will be measured by turnaround time and customer satisfaction rating
- To recommend changes to the bottle manufacturing process, so that product quality improves. Team success will be measured by reject rate and cost reduction
- To develop an action plan that addresses employee dissatisfaction in three areas – bonus plans, performance review and flexible working – that were identified in the latest annual employee satisfaction survey. Team success will be judged by securing the Board's agreement to implement the plan.

While the weighting issue discussed in work teams and project teams theoretically applies to ad hoc teams, in my experience most organisations opt for an overall assessment of what's been achieved in relation to the agreed terms of reference.

Incorporating team competencies[2]

While everyone agrees that team success should be measured in terms of "results", opinions about whether "how results are achieved" should be measured (and rewarded) differ. The Together Company believes strongly that "how" is important and it does so because the desired results are achieved only by team members having the right competencies and behaving in appropriate ways – within the team, between teams and between the team and other groups of people, for example customers and suppliers.

The "how" dimension may or may not vary with type of team, depending on whether there are specific behaviours and competencies that your organisation wants to encourage universally. These are often called "core team competencies or behaviours" such as:

- Encourage and support team colleagues
- Put team results before personal agenda
- Keep to agreed team processes
- Adaptable to perform different roles in the team
- Build relationships between the team and its customers, internal and external
- Share own knowledge freely with colleagues.

The development of an appropriate competency framework that can be applied to all types of teams in The Together Company was explored in Chapter 3, Performance management.

Competencies have to be measured of course. One of the simplest ways to do this is to measure, on say a ten-point scale, the number of times team members display the required competencies and behaviours. The scale could run from 1= rarely, to 10= all the time. If the team manager is doing their job properly, they're in a good position to observe what's happening. Alternatively, you could use 360 degree feedback (Chapter 4, Fair performance review) which includes the views of colleagues, other departments and perhaps customers, to obtain a more rounded view of the team's performance.

Step 4: Defining the payment method

There are two (sometimes conflicting) demands here: an adequate financial reward and affordability. The size of financial reward must provide an adequate incentive for team members to deliver what's required. That depends on team members' motivations and their current pay: if the financial reward is too small, it won't affect their behaviour at all; if it's too large, it may lead team members to focus entirely on the money at the expense of everything else. Affordability, the second demand, must balance budget requirements and market forces – what the competition pays (Chapter 6, Understanding your employment market: pay and benefits).

When it comes to how the "pay pot" is distributed in The Together Company there are five main choices, each of which is described below.

Percentage of salary

This is the most popular choice because it's easy to understand and it's assumed to reflect the relative market worth of each job in the team. However, not everybody (including me) would agree that an individual earning a base salary of £25,000 automatically has a higher worth to the team than someone earning £18,000. In your organisation's customer service teams for example, who has the greatest impact on customer satisfaction – the advisors or the managers? Does reward reflect the relative contribution of each group?

However, when work teams are made up of people doing different levels of work and they command widely different market salaries, a percentage of salary is often the most practical way to distribute rewards, and in the eyes of many employees, the fairest.

Lump sum

Paying the same lump sum, for example, £500 to all team members, assumes that each member makes the same level of contribution. In reality, that's rare. But lump sums can work well when the majority of team members carry out the same tasks and receive the same, or almost the same, base salary. Lump sums also send the message "we're all in this together". However, when teams are made up of people doing different levels of work, lump sums favour employees earning less than the average salary for the team. This "lack of equality" may be perceived to be unfair by higher earners in the team.

Percentage of salary and a lump sum

If the team includes large numbers of employees who are among the lowest paid in your organisation, combining percentage of salary and a lump sum is worth considering. This could work in the following way:

- When target performance (which I shall call 100) has been reached a lump sum payment of say £300 is awarded to everybody.
- Achievements above 100 are rewarded as a percentage of individual base salary.

Employees must feel that the point at which payment changes from lump sum to percentage of salary is "reasonable and fair". Employees on lower than average salaries should feel they are being rewarded "as equals" and employees on above average salaries, should feel their reward matches their contribution.

Team members' discretion

This involves giving team members some degree of freedom to decide how rewards should be distributed. The team, collectively, might suggest differential payments, but strict guidelines on how this will operate should be put in place to prevent dominant people getting the most and destructive peer pressure occurring. I advocate this approach only for well-established, self-managed teams whose members are used to working with one another, know what's expected of their colleagues, know what and how each person has contributed to the team, and trust each other to make fair judgments about reward.

Team leader's discretion

This involves giving the team leader total or some degree of freedom to decide how rewards should be distributed. If total discretion is to work, team members must have complete trust in the team leader to act fairly – and if a scheme applies to several teams, consistency between team leaders is crucial to that trust and fairness. Managers or business leaders who are responsible for several teams need to ensure that happens.

Team performance: raising the bar

The Together Company encourage teams to review their own performance and strive to achieve excellence in everything they do. Seven questions to guide a team discussion are given below:

- What have we learned and how have we developed as a team? (This should help open up a discussion of problems encountered and how they can be anticipated next time).
- As a team, how well have we performed? What stood out, positively and negatively?
- How efficiently have we used our time and resources, including time spent on irrelevancies?
- How can each of us help raise the performance of other team members and our own?
- To what extent are all team members' ideas considered and how free does each of us feel to speak our mind? (This should provide invaluable insights about the development of each person and the team as a whole).
- How well have we reacted to changing demands placed on us by managers or customers?
- What three things will we do next time to improve our performance?

Resolving the four problems about rewarding team excellence

Four common problems account for most of the reasons why rewarding team excellence is not as straightforward as first thought. Here are some practical tips for resolving them.

Problem 1: Individual contributions vary

It's important to remember that payments go to individuals and individual contributions are likely to vary. How will you handle this issue? You may decide that even if individual contributions vary, it would be de-motivating for the majority of team members to single out people for special payments – which of course, will be higher or lower than the average for the team. By not differentiating between individuals, you convey to team members: "We share responsibility for what the team has to achieve, so we share collectively the rewards of success and nobody should be singled out for special treatment".

On the other hand, you may feel that "individual performance or "special contribution" should be rewarded above the norm. Does that also mean poor performers will receive a lower bonus or maybe, no bonus? Who makes those decisions? Management might do so on the basis of individual performance reviews made by the team leader. Feedback from customers, internal and external, might help make informed judgments too. However, reward for individual contribution may convey the message that "individual contribution is more important than collective responsibility for team success". This downside can be overcome relatively simply by incorporating team and individual based performance measures into the scheme. Everybody takes responsibility for team performance measures and individual team members may have additional measures which relate to specific tasks or personal competency / behavioural requirements.

So, how does The Together Company resolve the often conflicting demands of rewarding team success and rewarding individual contribution? It doesn't have a "one size-fits-all" solution; that simply doesn't work because circumstances differ. Figure 8.2 shows an example of what can be done to address this issue.

FIGURE 8.2   Team bonus: allowing for individual contributions (% of base pay)

Performance measure	Team Leader		Team Member	
	Target	Max	Target	Max
Team Results – financial / non-financial	3%	6%	2%	4%
Individual Results – objectives / competencies	3%	6%	2%	4%

Problem 2: Time commitments and roles in project teams vary

The role of individuals and their time commitment to a project team often varies. Some individuals may be involved in a small part of the project, say 10%, some may be involved in several parts of the project, say 50%, while others are involved in 100% of the project. Part-timers may be working on more than one project at any given time or they may continue to do their "regular job".

Clearly this has reward implications. Figure 8.3 gives an example of bonus opportunities for a 12 month project, where target bonus varies with the role performed and time spent on the project[3].

FIGURE 8.3   Bonus linked to project role and time on project

Project role	Time on project	Target bonus (% of salary)
Project Manager	12 months	20%
Team Leader	12 months	12%
	9 months	9%
	6 months	6%
	3 months	3%
Team Member	12 months	8%
	9 months	6%
	6 months	4%
	3 months	2%

As a result of part-time involvement, several employees probably report to more than one team leader or project manager during the year. Bonus should be based on their performance throughout the review period (a year usually) so team leaders/project managers must complete a fair performance review (Chapter 4) at the end of the project – for full time and part-time employees. Given the difficulty of getting some people to do this on a timely basis, strong leadership from business leaders is paramount if employees are to feel that their bonus reflects their total performance rather than just part of it – good or bad.

Problem 3: Project team timescales vary

Project timescales vary enormously, from a few months to several years in for example, research and development departments or construction projects. That means the ultimate success of a project team may not be apparent for a long time. But it's hardly fair to expect team members to wait that long before getting any reward or recognition, so it's important to reward and / or recognise success at key milestones along the way.

In addition, what happens when a project is finished ahead of schedule? Many large scale civil engineering construction projects, such as motorways or office developments, have financial incentives to complete the project early. These incentives can be based on criteria such as cost savings, client feedback or additional work won. But what should you do if the agreed completion date is missed? That depends on why it was missed. If it was entirely within the team's control, I wouldn't pay the final bonus; if it was outside their control or influence and they achieved everything else were required to do, I'd pay the bonus. When it's a little of both, paying a proportion of the target bonus seems fair.

Problem 4: Expecting to be rewarded
for being part of an ad hoc team

Simply being part of an ad hoc team shouldn't automatically justify any form of additional financial reward. If it does, I believe this sends entirely the wrong message – which is: "If you take part we'll give you a bonus, even though you'll spend only a few hours on the project each week and always within your normal hours". When that happens, people start to "expect" rewards for just about anything. However, taking into account an individual's contribution to an ad hoc team, along with their performance in all other aspects of their work, at the annual salary review seems fair to me. This doesn't mean they should automatically receive an above average salary increase but their contribution should be recorded and recognised appropriately.

Teams need non-monetary recognition too

The Together Company knows that it's not enough to rely entirely on financial reward. It provides lots of non-monetary recognition too. Managers give feedback at team meetings and business leaders publicly recognise teams for outstanding achievements. This might be done in various ways, such as posting a congratulatory message on the intranet site or on notice boards or in company newsletters, for all employees to see. A director might make a personal visit to the team to congratulate them and celebrate their success. This could be followed by a special occasion for the team, such as a dinner, a concert, a sporting event or going to a prestigious conference. The cost of such recognition may run into a few hundreds of pounds, but the motivational value to the employees is high and immediate.

Is it right for you?

The most appropriate way to reward team excellence depends on the extent to which people work in teams, the nature of the work they do, and to some extent organisational size. Examples of choices that might be made according to circumstances are set out below.

Small but growing organisation

Your organisation depends on everybody really working together. Without good co-operation between different departments, you won't achieve your plans for growth. There's a mixture of highly paid employees who work in individual specialist roles and relatively low paid employees in small work teams which carry out generalist or transactional roles.

Financially-based rewards are only likely to be motivational if they are of the profit sharing type (Chapter 10, Sharing financial success). However, you should ensure that team excellence is recognised in other ways. This might be for a team which has been nominated by other teams for building excellent working relationships across the entire organisation. You could give the team a sum of money for them to enjoy a day out or evening together, plus a personal thank you from the Leadership Team. Publishing this in customer communications would demonstrate, externally, your commitment to team excellence too.

Fairly large organisation

Your organisation is structured around lots of well-established work teams and many of them do similar work, such as claims processing, retail customer service or manufacturing assembly. Each work team has clearly defined performance objectives which are cascaded from your organisation's business plan and results are measured quarterly.

You might consider introducing a team-based reward plan for work teams. This could be linked to two, or at the most three, key performance measures, and reward performance quarterly. Different types of reward should be considered – people in some teams might be motivated by a cash bonus (the amount on offer will affect their motivation), while others may prefer vouchers and surprise awards. Finding out people's preferences would be a good move. Teams could be nominated for a "Team of the Year" award in recognition of outstanding performance. Giving more employees the opportunity to take part in ad hoc teams would develop teamworking skills more generally.

Project team / professional services based organisation

Your organisation is team-based and places a strong emphasis on people's knowledge, competence and key roles. Delivering outstanding customer service depends on people within a team working well together and on good cooperation between teams across the entire organisation.

This suggests a combination of rewards. You might introduce a reward plan based on project team performance and use either financial or non-financial rewards depending on what's likely to motivate team members. When an individual team clocks up a special achievement, such as winning a new customer, running a highly successful conference or designing some very innovative marketing material, a big thank-you from the leadership team and an all expenses paid team outing could be just what's needed. Cooperation between teams could be recognised by a "Project Team of the Year" award where teams nominate other teams. Such an award should be given for outstanding contribution to the business as a whole and for innovative solutions to customer requirements that significantly improved customer satisfaction.

High-tech organisation

Your organisation has lots of "individuals" who tend to work independently of each other – not always to the benefit of them or the business. You want to encourage teamwork throughout the organisation and in some areas move to self-managed teams.

You could start by piloting a work team-based reward plan in a couple of areas of the organisation where teamwork is a priority – that is, where you expect it will have a positive impact on key business results fairly quickly. A mixture of financial and non-financial rewards should be considered. Non-financial could include access to technology gurus, conferences or research into leading edge technology. Employees in individually-based roles within the team, who encourage colleagues or go out of their way to build excellent working relationships with other departments, could receive special recognition, perhaps as a result of being nominated by colleagues. Giving more employees the opportunity to take part in task forces would develop teamworking skills more generally.

Key points

- Rewarding team excellence delivers the message: "Teamwork is a core value of our organisation". But it will only succeed if it has the unconditional support of the leadership team.
- Teams differ in what they do – day-to-day work, project work or ad hoc problem solving. If rewards for team excellence are to have the desired motivational impact on employees, they must be tailored to what they do and what motivates them to give their best.
- Team members' behaviour affects working relationships within the team and between teams. If there are specific behaviours and competencies that your organisation wants to encourage universally, they should be rewarded – financially and / or non-financially.
- Payment scales convey powerful messages to employees. Make sure you convey the right message:
    - A percentage of salary says "The higher the salary, the greater the worth"
    - The same lump sum says "Everybody's contribution is valued equally"
    - A combination says…..? Make sure it says what you mean it to say.
- Project team roles, time commitment and timescales vary widely: reflect these in scheme design.
- Mix financial and non-monetary rewards – keep the element of surprise too.

CHAPTER NINE

Rewarding customer satisfaction

Rewarding customer service excellence at The Royal Bank of Scotland Group

"Performance Plus" is a team-based incentive plan that rewards employees in customer-service related roles for achievements in customer service and sales. The plan covers around 3,000 people in Royal Bank of Scotland and NatWest retail branches. For most employees, the plan pays out up to £3,200 per year. However, employees in some roles within the retail branch team have more opportunity to provide higher levels of customer service and generate sales, so the plan has multipliers that increase the payment for particular roles. There are various non financial rewards for customer service excellence too.

Performance measures

To keep the plan simple there are just two performance measures:

Customer experience: this is measured at each branch through a Customer Satisfaction Index (CSI), which is based on aspects such as employees' product knowledge, helpfulness and responsiveness. Data to calculate the CSI is gathered in a variety of ways, such as mystery shopping and questionnaires.

Customer value points sold: each product such as a mortgage, savings account or loan that the branch team sells to customers has a number of points. The financial value of these points is set centrally.

Payouts

Customer experience: the target is expressed as an improvement in the CSI. Payout works as follows:

- If the CSI improvement target is missed, there's no payout
- When performance reaches target and above, there is a sliding scale of payments.

Customer value points sold: points sold by the whole team are expressed as a percentage of the minimum target. Payout works as follows:

- If performance is below target, there is no payout
- When performance reaches target and above, there is a sliding scale of payments.

Rewarding customer satisfaction
At a glance

How do you feel after you've stayed at a hotel where you were treated like a VIP? Great, relaxed and happy! You book a return visit and you tell your friends about it. How do you feel after visiting a retail store where the sales representatives treated you as an "inconvenience" they had to deal with? Annoyed, dissatisfied and negative! You tell your friends and they tell other people too. Next time, you and they, shop elsewhere!

If you want to understand how customers feel about your organisation you have to use the same criteria that they use to make that judgment. Take a train company, for example. You can ask lots of questions about cleanliness, the range of sandwiches, the colour scheme in the coaches and the frequency of services, and get good scores. But, if punctuality and the cost of fares matter a lot to customers and you don't include them in your questionnaire, you won't get a measure of how satisfied or dissatisfied they feel. Establishing customers' views about products and services comes naturally to The Together Company. It's crucial to understanding what customers want and value, and to securing the customer loyalty that leads to long term growth and business success.[1]

Who delivers that customer satisfaction and loyalty? Employees do, of course, by adding value through their product or service expertise, new ideas, efficient /

competent service (they know what they are doing!), building relationships with customers (they actually think like a customer) and promoting your organisation's products and services.[2] That's why The Together Company rewards customer satisfaction.

Setting the right course

Absolute clarity about three issues is the key here. The issues are:

- Being clear about outcomes
- Being clear about who to reward
- Overcoming barriers to success.

Being clear about outcomes

Fundamentally, this is about focusing employees' efforts on the things that matter most to customers. Perhaps many of your organisation's customers appear satisfied with the level of customer service, but after a couple of years they defect to a competitor. You find that baffling because they often talked to you about their desire to build a long term relationship with your organisation.

The actions you need to take to turn this situation around and build customer loyalty should be the focus of reward. In this scenario, being clear about outcomes is also about getting this right in relation to the "right" customers. Is this particular customer going to be profitable for your organisation in the future? If the answer is "yes", you need to set targets for revenue growth. But achieving the target will depend on building the right working relationship with your customer – if that doesn't happen you won't get the desired profitability for your organisation. I'll illustrate this point with an example. Imagine two employees, Jim and Sophie. Jim always takes short cuts to meet performance objectives ahead of time, but doesn't build any lasting relationship with key customers, so profitability plateaus and he always has to look for new customers. Sophie always delivers just on time and takes time to really understand her customer's business and what they want from your organisation. She often gets repeat business and referrals, and profitability has steadily increased. Who would you rather employ?

Being clear about who to reward

Who should you reward? The answer is the employees who actually deliver, directly or indirectly, the outcomes you've just selected, such as revenue growth and new business. Front-line customer facing employees who have a direct impact on customer relationships will be at or near the top of list, with their team leaders and managers close behind.

But what about all those other employees who are involved in designing, developing, marketing and manufacturing products, or meeting and greeting visitors or telephone callers, or preparing reports for clients. Don't they affect customer satisfaction too? Of course they do! Their input is there, but it's not always visible to the customer and that's the crux of it. Their input can be difficult to measure, but, and it's a huge but, many organisations expect these employees to deliver excellence in everything they do, although they don't reward them for it – financially or non-financially. This is completely opposite to The Together Company which strives continually to ensure that all employees who contribute in some way or other to customer satisfaction are rewarded and recognised appropriately.

Overcoming barriers to success

Employees may have heard on the grapevine that you're thinking about linking reward and customer satisfaction. How will they react? "Is this instead of the annual pay increase?" they may ask. "What happens if we don't meet the target? Will my base salary be reduced?"

Employees must believe there's something in it for them and that it's not a management ploy to reduce salary costs, for example. So, if you want to go ahead with a scheme, it's critically important to be up-front with employees who will be affected. Prepare some examples of how a possible scheme could work and some questions and answers around the following aspects:

- The reasons for wanting to link reward and customer satisfaction
- Possible targets and how they will be established and agreed
- How performance against targets will be measured
- Potential payments employees could receive.

One of the best ways to gain employees' confidence in what you want to achieve is to involve them in the design process. Employee focus groups, face-to-face meetings, a project team or a "pulse survey" are great opportunities to tap into employees' knowledge, ideas and concerns, and design the type of scheme that will work best in your organisation.

Measuring and managing targets

The Together Company has a robust process for measuring and managing customer-related targets. It's based around what I call the 5 KRAs – key result areas.

The first KRA: Developing the right targets

These should come directly from "being clear about outcomes". So, if your organisation wants to improve customer loyalty, for example, it needs to find out what factors affect customer loyalty. These might be quality of service delivered at the time of sale, post sales support, such as speed of complaint resolution and technical support, and customer involvement in new product design. These factors alone should determine your targets.

The second KRA: Cascade targets to the right level

Targets must always relate to aspects that employees can control or influence. That may sound obvious, but I come across many instances where employees just don't feel they can affect the outcome. So, targets need to be cascaded to the right organisational level, such as business unit, department, branch or team. That means actual performance in relation to those targets must be measurable at those organisational levels too. This is especially important for schemes that combine targets which apply to specific parts of the organisation and other targets which are common to all parts of the organisation.

The third KRA: Having SMART targets

Needless to say, The Together Company has SMART targets – specific, measurable, agreed, realistic and timed (Chapter 3, Performance management). A simply stated target, for example, "increase customer satisfaction in our 5 most profitable customers from 75% to 80%, over the next 12 months", is far better than a woolly statement of intent. The timescale must be realistic too: if it's too short, employees may feel they've been "set up to fail"; if it's too long, keeping them motivated may be difficult.

The fourth KRA: Measuring how targets are achieved

This is about how employees achieve their SMART targets – their behaviour and competence in doing their job. Aspects that are important to customers might include professionalism, responsiveness, helpfulness and attentiveness. There are many ways these aspects can be measured, such as asking customers to fill in a simple questionnaire, using mystery shoppers, getting input from team colleagues and, of course, team leaders and managers observing behaviours. Doing this at the appropriate organisational level is essential.

The fifth and final KRA: Giving feedback and coaching

Employees want to know how well they are doing, especially when part of their pay may be at risk, so managers must demonstrate they are totally committed to improving customer satisfaction by giving specific, relevant and constructive feedback about progress towards targets. This isn't optional; it's imperative. The Together Company uses private and public recognition of excellent customer service because it's a good motivator and encourages people to be as good as they can be. Chapter 13, Recognition and celebration, sets out the key steps to successful recognition. Highlighting low performance by giving only negative feedback – and in my experience that still happens far too often – is counter-productive. Disparity between what the organisation says and what it does is all too apparent to employees.

Making a customer service pledge

Securing the customer loyalty that leads to long term growth and business success is, of course, not just about rewarding customer satisfaction. It's about a culture where people "do best what matters most to customers" and they are happy to be judged accordingly. ABB Engineering Services (ABB ES), a project-based engineering consultancy delivering solutions to major client organisations in the chemicals, pharmaceuticals, oil and gas industries, has set out a Customer Service Pledge under the banner ABB "Always Being Brilliant" (Figure 9.1).

FIGURE 9.1   ABB Customer Service Pledge

We all deliver a brilliant service for our customers by:

- Actively seeking and nurturing relationships
- Listening to what they are asking for
- Making them feel valued
- Keeping our promises
- Always using positive language
- Caring as much about the customer service we provide, as the technical solution we deliver
- Supporting and coaching each other to Be Brilliant

In support of its Customer Service Pledge, ABB ES formed a group of "Always Being Brilliant Ambassadors" with a 90 day action plan that:

- Created a group determined to build customer loyalty
- Established a culture of celebrating success
- Provided guidance on house style for answering the phone
- Made available Brilliant Customer Service events to all personnel
- Supported colleagues to deliver their 90 day action plans.

Is it right for you?

What sort of scheme might suit your organisation? This will depend on several factors: its size, structure, systems for measuring customer satisfaction and employees' attitudes. Examples of the choices in different types of organisation are given below.

Small but growing organisation

Your organisation needs everybody to pay attention to detail in every aspect of customer relationships and because it's a small organisation, departments must work together closely to get things done successfully, so everybody has responsibility for creating a quality "customer experience". You could consider a scheme along the following lines:

Single measure of customer satisfaction: you set a minimum target and assess, annually, how easy or difficult it was to achieve.
Same payout for all employees: everybody gets for example, 2% of base salary or £500 for an increase in customer satisfaction from say 82% to 84%. If the target is

exceeded, you could make an additional discretionary payment of up to £250.

However, the scheme wouldn't reflect the relative contributions of departments, teams or individuals, so some people may feel their efforts aren't rewarded sufficiently.

Fairly large organisation

Your organisation has lots of work-based teams that interact with customers. Your customer relationship management and HR systems are reasonably sophisticated. For example, a customer satisfaction index has been developed for some business units and employee performance review is well established and respected. However, customer satisfaction varies by department or team so, ideally, any link to reward should take this into account. You could develop a scheme along the following lines:

- **Measure the drivers of customer satisfaction:** rather than having one measure of customer satisfaction at business unit level, you could break this down into the factors that drive satisfaction, such as the expertise, professionalism and helpfulness of employees.
- **Measure each team's contribution:** you could calculate a customer satisfaction index for each department (or team if appropriate) by averaging the scores for all factors (Figure 9.2). If you know the importance customers attach to each factor, you could calculate a weighted index, probably quarterly. You would need to survey a minimum of 100 customers and aim to increase this to 200 to improve the "statistical validity" of the results.
- **Differentiate reward by department or team:** you could calculate payments using a simple scale (Figure 9.3). Let's assume the minimum target customer satisfaction index by department is 75. That means employees in department C, with an index of 71, don't receive any payment. You need to tell them why and agree priorities for improving their contribution. Employees in the other three departments receive a bonus of 0.5% of base salary for every 1% above the target Satisfaction Index of 75. This means that employees in department D receive a 3.5% bonus, in department B, a 5.3% bonus and in department A, a 7% bonus.

FIGURE 9.2   Measuring customer satisfaction by department

| | | Factor scores (attributes of employees) | | | | Satisfaction Index (un-weighted average) |
	Expertise	Professionalism	Responsiveness	Friendliness	Helpfulness	
A	9.4	7.9	9.1	8.5	7.5	85
B	8.1	8.3	8.2	8.5	7.7	82
C	7.4	7.4	7.1	6.7	6.8	71
D	8.2	7.2	8.6	8.6		79

(Department)

FIGURE 9.3   Differentiating rewards by department

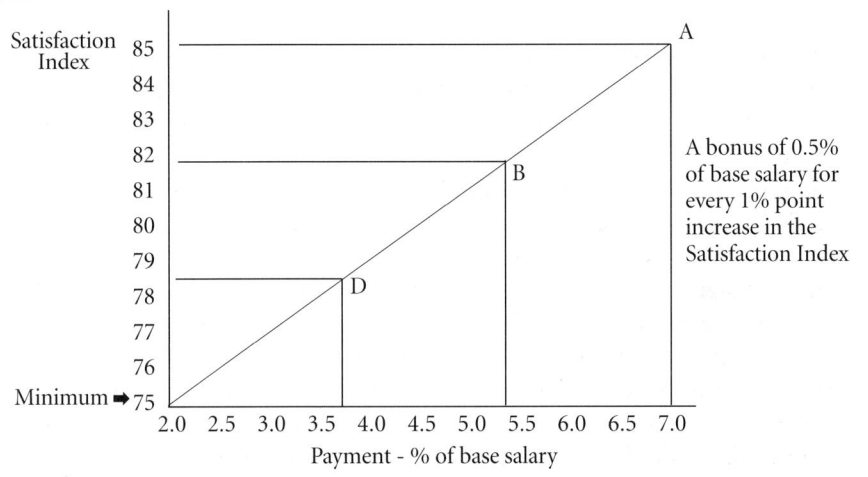

A bonus of 0.5% of base salary for every 1% point increase in the Satisfaction Index

The scheme gives higher rewards for higher performance and conveys the message "Continuous improvement counts". However, division between departments or teams that need to work together could arise. If cooperation is important, rewards should be based on a combination of team and department results.

Project team-based organisation

Your organisation is largely project-based and while each project is self-contained all projects contribute to business results of the entire organisation. Performance measures, which include customer satisfaction, are established at the outset of each project and actual performance is assessed at the end, using input from customers. However, you know that customer satisfaction (and ultimately customer loyalty) in relation to projects is based more on the experience of the relationship between the team and the customer, than solely on the quality of "the product / service" or work undertaken by the team. Customer feedback tells you this is where project teams need to improve.

You might want to consider two approaches:

- A bonus linked to customer ratings of satisfaction measured against criteria that matter most to customers, such as professionalism, problem resolution, relationship building and responsiveness. The bonus might be part of a plan which includes other performance criteria, such as cost and on-time delivery.
- All teams could compete for "Project Team of the Year" an award based on overall contribution to the entire organisation. The fact that different projects may have different degrees of difficulty would need to be taken into account. Difficulty might be assessed in terms of factors such as, technical challenge, resources available and balancing the needs of different groups of people involved. The "prize" could be presented jointly by a key customer and the Managing Director of your organisation.

High-tech / professional services organisation

Your organisation is for example, a software house, renowned for delivering high quality, bespoke software packages to prestigious customers or a professional services company such as lawyers or consulting engineers. But while your organisation gets customer accolades, the employees who develop the innovative software, provide engineering solutions, or give outstanding advice, feel left out.

You could of course, take into account an exceptional individual contribution to customer satisfaction (supported by evidence of course) when you review salaries. Alternatively, an award of shares or share options could be well received.

But, in my experience financial rewards often have limited value in terms of individual motivation for technology/professional services people and, if they are given, they need to be backed up by other forms of reward. Here are four examples that could prove motivational for somebody (or a team) who has received especially positive feedback from a prestigious customer:

- The opportunity to attend a hospitality event organised by the customer
- Opportunity to work on a new and challenging project
- Opportunity to represent your organisation at a leading-edge conference

- An expenses-paid week-end away.

All teams could compete for "Customer Champion of the Year" an award based on outstanding contribution to the business success of a customer. The "prize" could be presented jointly by a key customer and the Managing Director of your organisation.

Key points

- Reward the things that your customers tell you matter most to them – not what you "think" matters.
- Focus on the people who can actually deliver the desired outcomes. That might be everybody; it might be a few.
- Build grass-roots employee support for customer satisfaction related rewards, by involving them in the design process. This is a major factor in successful implementation.
- A strongly quantitative, but not overly complex, basis for gathering customer feedback is essential and employees must be able to trust it. Without trust, you'll quickly alienate employees.
- Make targets SMART. When they differ by organisational level, such as business unit, department, branch or team, it's vital they can be measured at the appropriate level. That way you connect employees' day-to-day work and customer needs.
- Give employees the opportunity to meet important customers in an informal setting and involve those customers in recognising employees for outstanding service.

CHAPTER TEN
Sharing in financial success

At a glance

Sharing in their organisation's financial success may not make employees work harder, but I believe it does draw their attention to the organisation's performance and the pay consequences for them. That alone may encourage employees to try to understand the business and consequently help to make them work smarter in the long term.

Not everybody, of course, shares this view. Critics of profit sharing for example, often say that people just don't understand how their day-to-day work affects the organisation's financial success; it's far too remote. When that happens, I believe the organisation, whatever its size, is completely failing to communicate to employees what matters most to their customers and shareholders.

According to the critics' logic, sharing in financial success should be more successful in smaller organisations, say with a few hundred or less employees. I disagree. If this is the case, why have Hewlett-Packard and John Lewis, both employing thousands of people, continued with profit sharing since they were founded? The answer is simple: in both companies, sharing financial success is a cornerstone of their business model, their ethos and their founding values.

HP's corporate objectives, which have guided the company in the conduct of its business since 1957, include the statements[1]:

- "Profit is the responsibility of all";
- "Everyone has something to contribute: It's not about title, level or tenure";
- "To help employees share in the company's success that they make possible".

The John Lewis Partnership is the UK's largest example of worker co-ownership. All permanent employees are Partners in the business and they share in its financial success. Figure 10.1[2] explains why.

FIGURE 10.1 The John Lewis Partnership: Sharing in success

"The supreme purpose of the John Lewis partnership
is simply the happiness of its members".
John Spedan Lewis

The 64,000 Partners of John Lewis and Waitrose don't merely have the satisfaction of working for a good business – they have the enjoyment of owning it. That is the essential difference at the John Lewis Partnership. The nature of this unique system of ownership is safeguarded by the Trusts under which John Spedan Lewis handed over the business to the staff.

Spedan Lewis aimed to create:

- A business that was fair to all – to customers and suppliers as well as to those who work in it
- A business that the Partners really felt was their own
- A business that would challenge and beat the competition and attract people at the top of their profession into its executive ranks.

Above all he wanted to instil in Partners an awareness that any benefits for them would depend entirely on the quality of the service they delivered to the customers and on the returns they were thus able to generate. As a keen student of history, Spedan Lewis was very conscious that almost all previous worker-cooperatives had failed because they lost sight of these commercial imperatives. He had no doubt of the need to maintain a tight commercial discipline and a sharp focus if the Partnership were to achieve its long-term objectives.

The Founder's aim was that the Partners should not just profit financially from the business but that they should enjoy the benefits of ownership in the broader sense – as he defined it *"the sharing of gain, knowledge and power".*

Every year a proportion of the business's profits are distributed to Partners as a percentage of their previous year's earnings. All receive the same percentage, irrespective of seniority and unit profit. In recent years, the bonus has varied between 12% and 15% and is set by the board as a judgment, rather than calculated by a fixed formula[3].

It is for these compelling reasons that The Together Company believes all employees should share in the financial success that they help create. This can be achieved in three main ways:

- Profit sharing schemes
- Share Incentive Plans
- Sharesave schemes – officially called SAYE Share Option Schemes.

Profit sharing schemes

A cash-based profit sharing scheme is probably the simplest way of enabling employees in The Together Company to share in financial success. This can be achieved by setting aside a proportion of the organisation's profits and distributing them, usually annually, to employees. Most cash-based profit sharing schemes cover all employees and there is no minimum number of employees before they become viable. They can work equally well in a restaurant with two partners, a software house with 100 employees or an engineering company employing thousands of people. In addition, a cash-based scheme can operate in any legal form of Together Company, such as publicly quoted or privately owned.

Publicly quoted organisations tend to use reported profits to calculate the profit pool which is distributed to employees. Privately owned organisations may choose a different method, depending on their structure and attitude to disclosure of profits. In both types of organisation one-off costs, such as write-offs or reorganisation costs, are usually excluded from the profit pool calculation and it's normal to specify a minimum level of profit before payments are made. Some schemes require the minimum to be exceeded before any payment is made and a proportion of profit above the minimum is set aside to create the profit pool.

Payments under cash-based profit sharing schemes differ hugely – 3% to 10% of salary is fairly typical, but 20% has been known. A percentage of salary (rather than an equal lump sum for everybody) is usually chosen on the grounds that it's easy to understand and it takes into account different job roles and levels of responsibility. However, some organisations challenge this notion of fairness and equity and vary the amount by an employee's performance rating. This is generally referred to as an "Individual Performance Factor". In my view, none of these approaches is better than the others. You should choose the approach that fits your culture.

Simple cash based scheme

An example of how this would operate is set out below:

- The bonus is based on profits before tax, providing the target profit is reached
- The minimum bonus is 5% of base salary or £750 (full time employees) whichever is the higher and will increase by 0.5% of basic salary for each £1m increase in profits above the target, to a maximum of 15% of salary
- 1 year employment service to qualify for the full payment (otherwise pro-rata).

Figure 10.2 gives potential bonus situations and the sums that would be payable. The line on the graph indicates how increases in profit will result in increases in the bonus payable. A bonus does not become payable until the target profit is reached – point A on the graph. The maximum bonus becomes payable when profit reaches £20m above the target – point C on the graph.

FIGURE 10.2   Cash - based profit sharing scheme

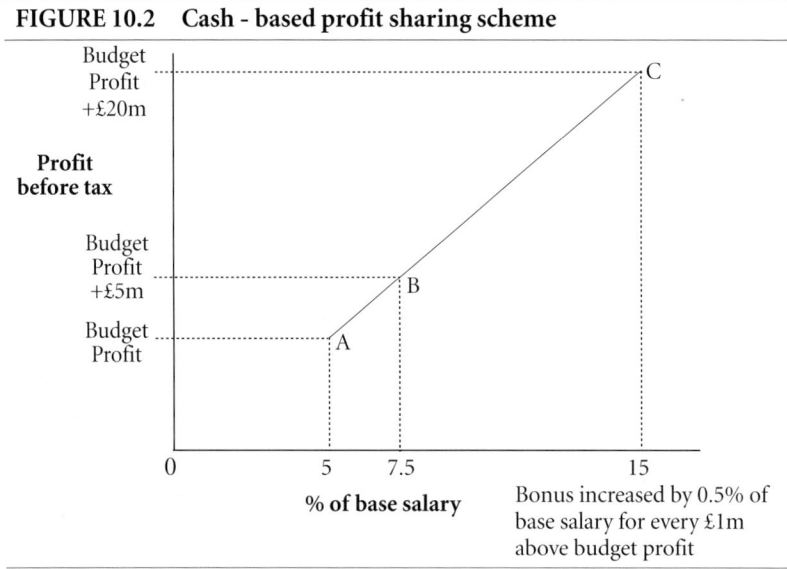

Figure 10.3 gives payments based on three scenarios: profit equals target; profit is £5m above target and profit is £20m above target.

FIGURE 10.3 Payments under a cash profit sharing scheme

Employee details	Employee 1	Employee 2	Employee 3
	Salary: £12,000	Salary: £7,000	Salary: £25,000
	Full time: 36 hours / week	Part time: 18 hours / week	Full time: 36 hours / week
	More than 1 year's service	More than 1 year's service	9 months' service
	Minimum bonus = £750	Minimum bonus = 18÷ 36 x £750 = £375	Minimum bonus = £750 x 0.75 = £562.50
Actual profit equals target	Calculated bonus 5% x £12,000 = £600	Calculated bonus 5% x £7,000 = £350	Calculated bonus 5% x £25,000 x 0.75 = £937.50
	Actual bonus = £750	Actual bonus = £375	Actual bonus = £937.50
Actual profit is £5m above target	Calculated bonus 7.5% x £12,000 = £900	Calculated bonus 7.5% x £7,000 =£525	Calculated bonus 7.5% x £25,000 x 0.75 = £1,406.25
	Actual bonus = £900	Actual bonus = £525	Actual bonus = £1,406.25
Actual profit is £20m above target	Calculated bonus 15% x £12,000 = £1,800	Calculated bonus 15% x £7,000 = £1050	Calculated bonus 15% x £25,000 x 0.75 = £2,812.50
	Actual bonus = £1,800	Actual bonus = £1050	Actual bonus = £2,812.50

Receiving shares or share options instead of cash

Many publicly owned companies which operate profit sharing schemes allow employees to buy shares in the company instead of receiving their profit share in cash. In the Royal Bank of Scotland's Group Profit Sharing scheme, shares that employees buy instead of taking the cash are held in trust and provided the employee keeps them for at least five years they don't have to pay income tax or National Insurance on the cash they've chosen to invest.

Starbucks takes a different approach to sharing in success and grants stock options instead of cash. Its plan is outlined in Figure 10.4.

Buying shares instead of receiving cash from a cash-based profit sharing scheme or receiving a grant of share options linked to company performance are not the only ways employees can share in the success of The Together Company. Two other share or share option based plans which enable employees to do just that, are described next.

FIGURE 10.4   Sharing Success at Starbucks – *Bean Stock*

At Starbucks, our success is defined, to a large extent, by the contributions of our partners. We want every Starbucks partner to share in the vision, the sense of pride and the financial success of Starbucks. *Bean Stock* is designed to give a broad base of partners the opportunity to own Starbucks' stock. With *Bean Stock*, partners have a personal connection to Starbucks' growth and a means of sharing in the financial rewards of the company's success. It is much more than just a stock option programme – it represents who we are as a business and it is why we call ourselves 'partners'.

> *If I hang my hat on one thing that makes Starbucks stand out above other companies it would be the introduction of Bean Stock. That's the name we gave to our stock option plan. With its introduction, we turned every employee into a partner.*
>
> Howard Schultz 'Pour Your Heart Into It'

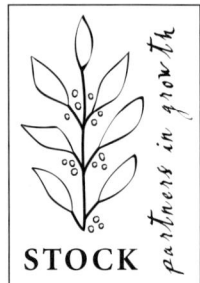

The grant of *Bean Stock* options is based on the company's performance and our efforts throughout the fiscal year. The grant is awarded as a percentage of the partner's earnings during the same fiscal year and given in the form of stock options. If held over three years from the date of grant, these stock options become tax efficient too.

This is a unique reward for a company within our industry sector, and especially as it is applicable to all partners (subject to eligibility), regardless of job role or seniority.

Share Incentive Plan

The share incentive plan[4, 5] (SIP) is a tax-advantageous, all-employee scheme that gives employees the opportunity to own shares in the company they work for. The introduction of SIPs was timed to coincide with the phasing-out of approved profit sharing schemes under UK legislation and SIPs operate alongside other all-employee share schemes, for example, Sharesave. A SIP can apply to Together Companies only if their shares are listed on a recognised stock exchange and a trust holds shares for employees who take part in the plan. A SIP can include four types of shares: free, partnership, matching and dividend.

Free shares

Up to £3,000 worth of free shares may be awarded to each employee each tax year, and if the shares are held for 3 years they are free of income tax. Free shares must be given on similar terms to all employees, for example three shares for each year of employment and five shares for each £1,000 of pay. Nothing comes out of an employee's own salary so take up rates in the companies who offer free shares are high, often above 90%. Employees don't have to accept free shares, although it's hard to see why they shouldn't.

Awards can be linked to performance and this may help overcome the concern of some business leaders that many employees view free shares as an "entitlement" rather than an encouragement to own shares. Performance conditions must be based on business results, either for the entire Together Company or part of it, and there's considerable flexibility over how performance conditions can be defined. However, employees must be told of them at the start of the plan – but what a great way of communicating what matters most to your organisation and to them.

Partnership shares

Employees are provided with the opportunity to invest pre-tax salary in shares and sell those shares after five years without any tax to pay. They can invest up to £1,500 per tax year (£125 per month) or 10% of salary – whichever is the lower – to buy partnership shares. The employee chooses how much to buy and at what intervals and the money is deducted from salary. Employees can stop buying partnership shares and restart at a later date. The median contribution is £80 per month and participation rates in the nine out of ten companies which offer partnership shares vary from 5% to 85% of employees. I suspect the wide variation comes down to three things: disposable income, effective communication and matching shares (see below).

Matching shares

Under a SIP, companies can give matching shares for each partnership share an employee buys, but why would you? Just look at supermarkets: Buy One – Get One Free, definitely works. When organisations give matching shares participation rates rise typically to 40% or more. The ratio of matching shares to partnership shares must not exceed 2:1 and it can be notched, for example, 1:1 for up to 100 shares and 2:1 up to 200 shares. As with free shares, no income tax or national insurance is payable when matching shares are awarded, but they must be held for at least three years.

Dividend shares

Employees taking part in a SIP are shareholders, so they receive dividends. It's possible to allow an employee to use up to £1,500 worth of dividends in any tax year to buy further shares (dividend shares) in the company and they must be held for three years. Around 50% of companies allow this; perhaps the others believe that cash payment is a regular reminder of the benefits of a SIP.

Sharesave

Sharesave schemes can apply to quoted and unquoted Together Companies. One of the main differences between Sharesave and SIP is that employees in Sharesave enter into a savings contract and are given a share option, that is, the right to buy a certain number of shares in the company they work for, at a fixed price, after 3, 5 or 7 years. An employee can save between £5 and £250 per month through a bank or building society and earn tax-free interest. For the 7 year option, savings are made for 5 years only with the savings remaining in the account for the further two years. In addition to earning interest, an employee receives a tax-free bonus after 3, 5 and 7 years.

Sharesave is popular for several reasons:

- The share price is fixed when the employee starts saving and can be up to 20% below the market value at that time
- Employees can withdraw their savings at any time
- Employees don't have to buy the shares. For example, if the share price at the end of the savings period has fallen below the fixed price, the employee could decide not to buy the shares.

Sharesave schemes are specifically designed to encourage wide share participation and about 50% of employees who are eligible to take part, do. They save, on average, about £70 per month (only slightly less than the median contribution to SIPs).

Tesco has operated sharesave schemes for 25 years. In February 2006, Tesco announced "employees share £111m save-as-you-earn windfall" after two sharesave schemes matured.[6] Employees, from shop assistants to senior managers, who invested in the supermarket's three-year scheme, will have nearly doubled the value of their savings because Tesco shares have risen by 98% over the past three years. Employees who invested in the five-year scheme will have seen a 59% increase in the value of shares since the scheme was launched. Interestingly, around two-thirds of employees chose to hold on to their shares rather than cash them in.

Case Study

Employee Share Acquisition at ABB

ABB, the Swiss-owned global engineering company, has recently introduced its own share acquisition plan for its employees world-wide. It's an opportunity for employees to purchase a stake in ABB Ltd., to invest in their joint future and success.

The plan is a voluntary share ownership programme, providing employees with the opportunity to save part of their monthly salary over a 12 month period to eventually buy ABB Ltd shares. In general, all full-time and part-time employees are eligible to participate.

The plan is offered in 40 of the countries where ABB operates and ABB shares are traded in Swiss Francs. The plan's key features are set out in Figure 10.5. Although these features apply to the first issue of the plan, ABB may decide to release further issues of the plan, on a 12-month rolling basis. Participation rate in the UK is 24%.

FIGURE 10.5 ABB Employee Share Acquisition Plan

Plan objectives

- Provide the opportunity for employees to become a shareholder and participate in the growth and success of ABB
- Increase employees' identification with the ABB Group, its targets, objectives and results.

Key features of UK plan

- A savings based plan where permanent employees can save up to 10% of monthly salary up to a maximum of £330 per month
- Employees must save for a defined 12 month period, at the end of which they earn interest on their savings, although if the employee withdraws the savings before 12 months, they lose the interest
- The savings are held on employees behalf by a Trustee in a bank and because the plan operates in several countries, savings are in local currency, which eliminates all currency risks
- At the end of the 12 months savings period employees have the choice to:
  - Keep the shares in the Employee Share Account where dividends are re-invested in additional shares
  - Sell their shares at any time and receive the proceeds
  - Transfer their shares to their own brokerage account
- The share offer price, at which shares can be purchased at the end of the 12 months, is fixed at the start of the savings period
- If an employee chooses to buy ABB shares, they will be liable for income tax on savings interest or any share gain. They may be liable to Capital Gains Tax on the shares, when sold.

Practical example

Employee saves £50 per month, so total savings over 12 months =	£600
Savings converted to Swiss Francs @ 2.28 CHF/£ =	CHF1,368
Number of shares (assuming Share Offer price is CHF 6.5) =	210
10% adjustment for interest and currency exchange, so number of shares =	231
Number of shares is rounded up to nearest 10 shares, so final number of shares =	240

Is it right for you?

How would profit sharing or share ownership fit your existing culture, or help shape a new one? How would it fit the profile of the existing workforce and your wider strategies for recruitment and retention? Examples of choices in different organisational circumstances are set out below.

Small but growing organisation

Your organisation is fairly small in terms of numbers of people, but is growing steadily and profits have been rising. The Leadership Team believes that "everybody" contributes to business success and it wants to continue building an engaged and talented workforce. A cash-based profit sharing scheme, in which everybody participates, would be a good starting point. Employees could share in a pot of money, for example a percentage of company profits, when the "expected" target has been reached. You might decide that everybody should receive an extra half a month's salary, but if an "ambitious" profit target is reached, the payment will be an extra full month's salary.

Fairly large organisation

Your organisation employs a wide range of people, many of whom are low paid compared to the UK average, but there are pockets of high earners too. You are keen to build loyalty and many competitors don't offer any form of profit sharing.

Sharesave is likely to be popular with your low paid employees who can't afford to take risks with their regular savings. They are in a no-lose situation: if the share price goes down, employees can simply choose to get their money back with interest; if the shares increase in price, employees enjoy the upside.

A SIP would be worth considering too, although the cost of drawing up rules, setting up a UK trust, and getting shareholder and HM Revenue and Customs approval, is likely to be an important factor in arriving at a decision.

High earners should find Sharesave and SIP attractive investment opportunities. If the cost of setting up Sharesave or SIP is unacceptable, you should consider a cash-based profit sharing to demonstrate to employees how their contribution and your organisation's business success are inextricably linked.

Project-team based organisation

Your organisation consists mainly of average or above average earners, who have knowledge and skills which enables them to move easily between different types of organisation.

A cash profit sharing scheme, with the option to invest in shares instead of taking cash, coupled with a SIP and / or Sharesave scheme could be especially attractive to them. The cash-based plan gives employees cash-in-hand which they can use in the short-term and the share-based plans provide opportunities to accumulate wealth in the medium term – and take some of the gains along the way. The share-based schemes are likely to be affordable for many people too. Take someone on a salary of £30,000 for example, who saves £200 per month (£2,400 a year) in Sharesave – that's 8% of salary, which is not much more than the average employee contribution (6%) to lots of pension schemes.

High-tech / professional services organisation

Your organisation has a large proportion of high earners, who have knowledge and skills which are highly sought after. You are very keen to retain these people – who are expensive to replace (around £15,000 each). They like having a "slice of the action", so having a SIP which gives matching shares could be an attractive opportunity for them to build up a stake in your organisation as it grows and prospers. An offer of free shares would benefit all employees – not just high earners – and could be a competitive differentiator.

Sharesave will be affordable for many employees too. For someone on a salary of £50,000, who saves £250 per month (£3,000 a year) in Sharesave, this is 6% of salary, which compares favourably with the average employee pension contribution in many schemes.

Key points

- Profit sharing or share ownership may not make employees work harder, but it may help them work smarter. That's got to be good for customers and shareholders and ultimately, profits.
- Enabling employees to share in the financial success of your organisation is about business leaders believing they should. They must believe everybody contributes to organisational success – albeit in different ways and to different degrees. After all, your organisation will succeed only through the actions of employees.
- Share ownership offers employees potential tax breaks and National Insurance savings – why make them pay more when you don't have to?

CHAPTER ELEVEN
Rewarding business leaders

Aligning senior management reward and performance at BAA[1]

BAA is the world's leading airport company. It owns and operates seven UK airports and has management contracts or stakes in eleven airports outside the UK. BAA financed and built the £500 million Heathrow Express rail link from Heathrow to London Paddington and is developing Terminal 5 at Heathrow. BAA is a leading developer and manager of airport retailing.

In 2004, the Remuneration of the Board carried out a comprehensive review of reward arrangements of BAA's 1,200 senior managers, consulting extensively with key stakeholders and their representative bodies. The review led to changes in annual incentive bonus and deferred annual bonus plans, a new performance share plan which replaced the Employee Share Option Scheme plan and simplified annual salary review. The changes have been designed to achieve four things:

- To make rewards more performance-focused than before
- To link reward and the financial success of BAA
- To provide market-competitive rewards which reflect best practice; and
- To make reward processes transparent.

Reward and Recognition Manager, Julie Gregory, and her team have been at the forefront of the changes, designing new schemes, modifying existing ones and developing all communication materials. Julie explains:

"In the past, there was a black box element to salary review and bonus. People didn't

know how their salary increase and bonus were calculated and that led to lack of trust. The share option scheme no longer reflected BAA's strategic ambitions for long term growth and we needed an incentive plan that did. Now, our arrangements are very focused and transparent."

Establishing business-aligned performance targets

BAA uses a balanced scorecard approach to defining performance targets that includes financial performance targets and non-financial Key Performance Indicators (KPI). Company targets are cascaded, so that each operating or support unit, for example Heathrow Airport or Central Airport Services, have their own financial performance and KPI targets. A senior manager has up to six targets which are linked directly to their unit's targets. Financial performance and KPI targets are weighted between 20% and 80%, according to the manager's key areas of influence. A Managing Director of an airport, for example, will have greater influence and control over financial performance than senior managers in terminals who will have greater influence and control over KPI targets such as "security queuing".

Reviewing individual performance

Half yearly and end year performance reviews are mandatory, but BAA recommends quarterly reviews take place during the year. The performance review has two parts:

- Achievement against targets ("what" has been achieved and "how" it's been achieved). This feeds into the annual incentive bonus.
- Overall contribution in the role (the outcomes of work achieved, and the levels of skill and competence which have influenced these outcomes) which is not just about achievement against targets, but includes the impact made on the team or department and the level of competence used in handling the demands of the job. This feeds into the annual salary review.

The "how" element (the behavioural part) is reviewed against BAA's "Leadership and General Competency Framework", which applies to all employees, not just senior managers. The framework incorporates two different types of competencies:

- **Four leadership competencies:** be courageous, be curious, provide meaning and enable others
- **Seven general competencies:** focus on the future, change and improve, deliver for travellers and stakeholders, think and decide, focus on commercial success, deliver high performance and grow through learning.

360 degree questionnaire-based feedback helps inform the "how" part of the performance review. The feedback, which is given against the Leadership and General

Competency Framework, is obtained from the manager's line manager, peers, direct reports, as well as "internal" and (possibly) external customers.

A manager's overall contribution (the outcomes of work achieved, and the levels of skill and competence which have influenced these outcomes), is assessed against a

---

FIGURE 11.1   BAA: Ratings for overall contribution

Outstanding
- At your level, made the greatest contribution to the team or department's performance
- Created and taken advantage of opportunities that have had significant positive impacts
- Worked noticeably beyond the expected or required scope of your role for a substantial part of the year
- Overcame significantly difficult challenges to achieve exceptional results
- Been seen as a role model by peers and managers
- Added significant value to the business on a regular basis

Highly effective
- Consistently delivered some areas of notably high achievement against objectives and role accountabilities
- Dealt with unexpected challenges effectively
- Taken advantage of opportunities to work beyond the scope of your role
- Been the subject of consistently good feedback, and seen by peers and customers as a highly effective performer
- Developed solutions to move the team/department forward

Effective
- Delivered performance at the required level against objectives and role accountabilities
- Needed additional support in only one or two areas
- Worked consistently within the scope of your role
- Been the subject of good feedback from peers and customers

Needs improvement
- Not delivered against most objectives and role accountabilities
- Have plans in place in the next financial year to fill capability gaps which prevent effective performance
- Demonstrated some improvement in capability, but not considered effective

Unacceptable
- Not delivered against most or all agreed objectives and role accountabilities
- Not taken effective action in dealing with performance shortfalls
- Been the subject of unsatisfactory feedback, and have failed to respond to this during the year
- Not improved your capabilities
  Or
  Recently taken on the role and therefore still learning and developing

---

five-category rating scale (Figure 11.1). Ratings are calibrated across the business (for both 'overall contribution' and 'achievement against objectives') by groups of managers who meet to ensure that:

- The distribution of performance ratings looks sensible. BAA believes it is highly unlikely that 100% of a single team could all legitimately be classified as "Highly Effective" for example, so results like this are challenged. On the other hand, BAA does not "force fit" the expected distributions, as this could be unfair
- Benefits that are dependent on effective performance are applied appropriately
- BAA lives up to its aim of a high performance culture.

If a senior manager's rating changes as a result of calibration, their line manager discusses this with them and explains the reasons for the change.

Providing performance-linked and market-competitive salaries

A senior manager's starting salary is determined by their grade, the level of experience and skills, internal comparisons with colleagues doing similar work and the market range for the job, in other organisations. But subsequent increases are entirely performance-related. At the Annual Salary Review (ASR), BAA uses a "pay matrix" to determine whether or not a manager receives a salary increase. The matrix (an example is shown in Figure 11.2) combines the 'overall contribution' rating and salary market position.

FIGURE 11.2   BAA: Example Pay Matrix

Rating for "overall contribution"	Salary position in the market		
	If salary is currently below market median range, ASR increase will be in the range…	If salary is currently at market median range, ASR increase will be in the range…	If salary is currently above market median range, ASR increase will be in the range…
Outstanding	8% to 10%	7% to 9%	6% to 7.5%
Highly effective	5% to 7%	4% to 6%	3% to 4.5%
Effective	3% to 4.5%	2.5% to 3.5%	1% to 2.5%
Needs improvement	0% to 2%	0% to 1.5%	0%
Unacceptable	0%	0%	0%

This matrix is for illustrative purposes only and the percentages will change each year

BAA's policy is to pay an effective performer at "median" level in the relevant market for the job. The pay matrix is designed to help ensure that:

- A highly effective performer whose salary is below market median receives a larger than average increase
- An effective performer whose salary is already at the market median receives an average increase
- An individual whose performance needs improvement and whose salary already is above market median doesn't receive an increase.

Linking reward and business performance

Senior managers' rewards and BAA's success are linked at two levels: the operating or support unit where they work; and Company. This is achieved through an annual incentive bonus scheme and a performance share plan respectively.

Rewards for operating or support unit performance

The Senior Management Incentive Scheme is an annual bonus scheme designed to incentivise all senior managers and reward them for their contribution to meeting business objectives. A bonus pool, based on how well the operating or support unit has performed against its targets for financial performance and KPIs, is used to pay for bonuses to individuals. The size of pool varies according to level of performance achieved:

- "Stretch" performance for financial and KPI targets: 100% of the bonus pool is available
- "Target" performance for financial and KPI targets: 50% of the bonus pool is available
- "Below threshold" financial performance: no bonus is paid, regardless of KPIs and individual performance.

Half of the bonus pool is influenced by the manager's achievement against individual objectives as assessed at performance review, and half is not (unless performance is "unacceptable", when no bonus is paid). To enable BAA to incentivise and reward its high performers, a manager's share of the bonus pool is varied by a performance multiplier which works as follows:

- Outstanding or Highly Effective performers will receive an increased share of the bonus pool
- Effective performers (scoring 70%) will find their share of the bonus pool is unaffected
- Managers rated Needs Improvement will receive a decreased share of the bonus pool

●Managers rated Unacceptable will not receive a bonus.

A worked example of how the incentive scheme operates is set out in Figure 11.3. It's based on a manager working in Central Airport Services (CAS), on an annual salary of £40,000 and bonus potential of 25%. CAS financial targets and KPI targets are weighted 60:40 respectively.

FIGURE 11.3   BAA: Establishing the bonus pool

Financial performance – 80% achievement, so bonus pool is 80% x 60% weighting	48%
KPI performance – 50% achievement, so bonus pool is 50% x 40% weighting	20%
Total initial bonus pool	68%
Individual performance element = 50% x 68%	34%
Element not influenced by individual performance = 50% x 68%	34%
Impact of individual performance score if achieved 75% against individual objectives = 34% x 105% multiplier	35.7%
Share of the maximum bonus achieved = 34% + 35.7%	69.7%%
Bonus achieved (£40,000 x 25% x 69.7%)	£6,970

Rewards for Company performance

The Performance Share Plan is a long-term incentive plan where awards of BAA shares, rather than share options, are made to senior managers, at no personal cost. The shares are transferred to managers who participate in the plan provided that BAA meets agreed performance conditions, generally after three years. The Remuneration Committee decides each year whether awards are to be made and who is eligible to receive them. To be eligible a manager must be rated at least an 'Effective' performer. If an award is made, shares are allocated to a manager and held in the BAA Employee Share Trust generally for three years.

The number of shares awarded depends on three things: the value of award a manager is eligible to receive as a percentage of their base salary, BAA's share price and the company meeting an agreed performance condition which is based on BAA's Total Shareholder Return (TSR) relative to the TSR of a comparator group of 30 other companies (Figure 11.4). The companies have been chosen to reflect the business sectors in which BAA operates. TSR is the growth in share price plus the value of dividends received over the performance period, assuming all dividends are reinvested into new shares. The target is for BAA's TSR growth to rank a least 16th against its comparator group of companies for any awarded shares to be released. For 100% of awarded shares to be released BAA must rank 7th or higher. If BAA ranks 16th, 35% of awarded shares will be released. A sliding scale operates between ranked positions 7th and 16th.

FIGURE 11.4   BAA: The comparator group of companies

Regulated businesses and infrastructure management	BG Group, Centrica, International Power, National Grid, Transco Group, Scottish and Southern Energy, Severn Trent, United Utilities, Scottish Power
Retail	Boots Group, Dixons Group, GUS, Kingfisher, Marks & Spencer, Wm Morrison, J Sainsbury, Next
Business services	Rentokil Initial, Hays, Bunzl, Rexam
Property	Slough Estates
Tourism, travel and leisure	Arriva, British Airways, Carnival, Compass Group, First Group, Hilton Group, Intercontinental Hotels Group, Scottish and Newcastle, Whitbread

Encouraging Senior Directors to invest their own money in the business

The Deferred Annual Bonus Plan provides an opportunity for Senior Directors and above, to invest some or all of their after-tax Senior Management Incentive Scheme bonus in BAA shares and receive a Matching Share Award equal in value to up to 100% of the gross amount of bonus that is invested. If a Senior Director chooses to invest in the plan, the matching shares are held in the BAA Employee Share Trust, generally for three years. The number of Matching Shares depends on three things:

- The amount of earned bonus invested in BAA shares, up to a Personal Participation Level set by the Remuneration Committee
- The level of earned bonus as a percentage of maximum bonus potential
- The average of the mid-market closing prices for BAA shares over the three business days before the Award date.

BAA has set a corporate performance condition which must be satisfied in order for Matching Shares to be released. The performance condition is growth during the three year performance period in earnings before interest, tax, depreciation and amortization (EBITDA), above the Retail Prices Index (RPI). The number of Matching Shares released increases as performance increases.

A worked example of how the Deferred Annual Bonus Plan operates is shown in Figure 11.5. It's based on a Senior Director earning £100,000 and bonus potential of 50%.

FIGURE 11.5   BAA: Worked example incorporating performance condition

Earned bonus = 50% of maximum bonus potential = 25% of salary	£25,000
Gross deferred bonus (Maximum Personal Participation Level of 55% x £25,000)	£13,750
Income Tax / Employee NIC (currently 40% plus 1%)	(£5,637.50)
Net bonus used to purchase "Invested Shares"	£8,112.50
Number of Invested Shares purchased at share price of £6.00	1,352
Number of Matching Shares (£13,750/£6.00)	2,291
Extent to which corporate performance condition is achieved	50%
Number of Matching Shares to be released (2,291 x 50%)	1,145

Making reward processes transparent

BAA communicated the new reward arrangements in two ways:

- Briefing sessions – 3 slots per day, to explain to groups of managers the features of the new reward arrangement, how they differed from the previous ones and why
- Brochures – one for each of the four main reward elements: Annual Salary Review, Senior Management Incentive Scheme, Performance Share Plan and Deferred Annual Bonus Plan. Each booklet is designed in an easy-to-read question and answer style.

The Reward and Recognition Team used a simple questionnaire to evaluate the effectiveness of these communications. Julie Gregory comments:

"We've had some good feedback from senior managers about the way we've taken their views into account in designing the new arrangements and the way we've communicated them. The professionally-designed booklets have been particularly well received. In addition, performance against corporate performance (TSR) is displayed on the Reward and Recognition intranet site, so senior managers can see their potential share awards. That link between personal performance and Company results is highly tangible."

Rewarding business leaders
At a glance

Henry Mintzberg's article "Enough Leadership", in Harvard Business Review[2] was thought-provoking: *"Leadership, we all know what it is. It stimulates teamwork, takes the long view, builds trust and lots more."* So, are business leaders in your organisation rewarded for:

- Stimulating teamwork and demonstrating that they work as a team?
- Continuous improvement in the long term, not just short-term results?
- Building trust among customers, employees and investors?

The answers to these questions are about alignment of the interests of shareholders and those of business leaders. The lack of alignment has led many stock market-quoted organisations to introduce reward plans which require business leaders to build and maintain a significant shareholding in their organisation.

Shareholder objections at annual general meetings and disquiet among institutional shareholders about performance conditions attached to rewards are now commonplace. But despite the introduction of tighter performance criteria and more robust corporate governance, the reward packages for business leaders in many organisations still make uncomfortable reading. If I had ten pounds for every time I've heard business leaders tell me "yes, of course, we are committed to customer satisfaction" or "employee satisfaction is a top priority here" and neither feature anywhere in their reward package for business leaders, I'd be a millionaire.

So, how does The Together Company reward business leaders? I've grouped different types of schemes into four categories:

- Cash bonus plans
- Share option schemes
- Phantom share plans
- Long term incentive plans.

Cash bonus plans

Top management bonuses have rarely been out of the business headlines in the last 10 years. The controversy has been fuelled by big bonuses in organisations which shareholders believe have performed poorly. Bonuses always should be linked to the achievement of pre-determined targets for organisation performance, business unit performance, personal objectives or a combination. I say "should be" because I've come across several organisations where bonuses seem to be regarded as "part of the package" and have an extremely tenuous link to performance. This hardly sets a good example when the rest of the people in the organisation get an inflation-based pay rise.

Bonus varies widely by job, even within the same industrial sector. A Managing Director for example, might receive anywhere between 25% and 50% for meeting performance targets and 50% to 100% for exceeding them. For an absolutely outstanding performance, 200% might be awarded. Bonuses for business leaders reporting to the MD typically fall between 15% and 50%.

Not surprisingly, financial performance targets feature strongly in annual cash bonus plans. Frequently used measures include profit before tax, earnings per share growth, revenue growth and return on capital employed. But financial results are often the product of non-financial results, such as customer satisfaction or retention, employee satisfaction, the number of viable products in the pipeline and health and safety standards, so these are increasing in popularity.

Competition to retain the best business leaders has led many organisations to introduce a "deferred bonus plan". This enables business leaders to defer all or part of their annual bonus and receive such an award in the form of shares ("deferred shares") rather than cash. After a further period, for example three years, some organisations award business leaders additional shares for the deferred shares they hold. If the business leader leaves the organisation during this period all or some of the additional shares are forfeited.

Share option schemes

While the way share options are now accounted for in company accounts has deterred some organisations from continuing to use them as an incentive for business leaders, share options remain widely used by FTSE 350 companies. There are two main types of scheme open to The Together Company: Approved company share options and the Enterprise Management Initiative.

Approved company share options[3,4]

An approved (by HM Revenue and Customs) company share option scheme provides a tax efficient and flexible way to reward business leaders in Together Companies. Options can be awarded over the shares of UK private, public or listed companies and also over the shares of foreign parent companies. An approved scheme attracts income tax and National Insurance relief on options over shares worth up to £30,000 per employee, at the date of grant.

Options are granted at fair market value which, for a privately-owned Together Company, is agreed at the date of grant with HM Revenue and Customs. Historically, companies were required to limit all option grants to a maximum of four times salary. While this limit has been retained by several companies, grants of between six times and ten times salary have been made by some organisations. Many schemes were criticised for awarding most of the available share options at the start of the scheme without any regard for demonstrated performance. Now most companies phase grants of share options, typically at a rate of one or two times salary each year.

Gone are the days when share options were "taken for granted" and didn't depend on performance. Earnings per share growth relative to the RPI is by far the most popular performance measure, although total shareholder return (TSR) measured relative to a comparator group of companies, is gaining in popularity.

> **Total Shareholder Return (TSR)**
>
> A measure of company performance. TSR measures the return that a company has provided for its shareholders reflecting share price movements and assuming reinvestment of dividends.

Performance targets are certainly getting tougher. That's good. Targets which are easy to achieve lead to mediocre performance and share options become "an entitlement". The Together Company is totally committed to rewarding business leaders for performance and if performance falls short of expectations, so do rewards.

Although the link between share option awards and performance is strengthening, not all top business leaders are convinced that share options are an appropriate way to attract and reward talented business leaders today. This has led an increasing number of organisations to develop more creative reward schemes, for example long term incentive plans (see later).

Enterprise Management Initiative (EMI)

The EMI is a tax-efficient way for incentivising business leaders (and other key people) in smaller quoted or unquoted Together Companies. It provides particularly attractive reliefs from income tax, National Insurance contributions and capital gains tax. It's structured as a share option scheme, but unlike approved company share options, EMI options may be granted over shares worth up to £100,000 per employee. The £100,000 is an all-time limit, not per grant.

EMI options can, in principle, be offered at any exercise price (at fair value, above it or below it) and while there is no need to agree valuation with HM Revenue and Customs, it's usually advisable to do so. If the price is set below fair market value, income tax will be payable at exercise on the difference between the exercise price and fair market value.

Individual performance conditions can be attached both to the grant and exercise of options, which means EMI options can be used as powerful short term and / or medium term incentives. Options must be capable of exercise within 10 years of grant, but there's no statutory period before options can be exercised.

Any number of people may be included in an EMI, but there's an overall limit on the value of the shares of £3m per company. It's worth noting too, that if your organisation already has an approved company share option scheme, where the £30,000 limit has been used, only £70,000 is available to you under an EMI. In addition, anybody who directly or indirectly controls more than 30% of the ordinary share capital of the company is excluded from an EMI.

Many privately-owned Together Companies want to ensure that people in an EMI can convert their shares into cash without the company having to be sold or floated. This can be achieved by setting up an Employee Benefit Trust, which is a means for creating an internal market in the shares.

Phantom share plans

Phantom share plans[5] are a form of cash bonus scheme made to look like a share scheme. Such schemes will usually be established by a Together Company which isn't in a position to establish a share scheme, typically because it's a subsidiary of a listed company and doesn't have its "own" shares. The intention is to encourage business leaders (and sometimes other key people) to stay with the company and to improve its performance by providing a financial incentive to do so.

At the start of the plan a business leader is given an award which represents a specified number of shares (phantom) or units in The Together Company. A typical phantom share plan will mirror a real share plan by for example, using terms such as "grant of option" or "exercise of option" but it doesn't give participants (business leaders) any right to acquire shares. Instead, it promises to pay a cash sum which equates to the increase in value of notional-tracker shares between a starting date and a date when they can claim the cash bonus. The promise, like a real share award or share option, is usually subject to performance conditions that have to be met. These conditions might be "absolute" or "relative". Absolute conditions relate solely to specific business targets, for example, achieve a 20% increase in profit margin. Relative conditions relate to a comparator group of competitors, an increasingly common practice in approved company share option schemes and long term incentive plans.

Phantom share plans are classified as "unapproved" by HM Revenue & Customs, which rules out any special tax advantages. The cash payment received is taxable as earnings.

Long term incentive plans (LTIPs)

LTIPs[6] are now as popular as approved company share option schemes among larger companies. Around three-quarters of FTSE-100 companies and half of mid-250 companies have an LTIP in place. The underlying premise of an LTIP is to align the interests of business leaders and shareholders. This is a key objective of reward policy in The Together Company.

Most LTIPs have one or more of the following features:

- Performance share awards – awards of free shares which are based on the extent to which set performance targets are achieved over three or more years
- Deferred shares – an award of shares which is usually released after three years
- Matching shares – an award of additional free shares made if deferred shares are held for a specified period.

Unlike approved company share options schemes, LTIPs are confined mostly to directors and key business leaders. Awards from most LTIPs are in shares, not share options, and are linked primarily to TSR measured relative to a comparator group of companies. Awards usually depend on the company out-performing the comparator group. I've always liked this concept. Investors, like business leaders, choose companies where they believe they will get the best return. When the company wins, the business leader wins.

At the start of the performance period, The Together Company specifies an initial grant of performance shares which will be awarded if the performance conditions are met. If, at the end of the performance period, the performance condition is met and the business leader holds the performance shares for three years, the plan may award matching shares (these are additional free shares). The ratio between performance shares and matching shares is usually no more than 2:1.

Some schemes have a further twist, in that they award deferred shares as a means of retaining key business leaders and the number of shares doesn't vary or depend on the company's performance – only the business leader's continued employment. Deferred shares are usually acquired by the business leader investing their annual bonus in the LTIP, rather than taking it in cash.

The requirement for business leaders to build and maintain a significant shareholding in their company has focused minds. Shareholding policies vary from having a standard level of holding for example one times salary for all business leaders in the plan, to varying the amount by job level, for example, 200% of salary for the Chief Executive, 150% for other directors, 100% for other senior executives and 50% for senior managers. In some organisations business leaders who fail to meet the shareholding requirement either have their future awards reduced from the LTIP or receive no further awards at all.

Is it right for you?

Deciding how to reward business leaders depends primarily on two things: what you want to reward and the size and ownership structure of your organisation. Examples of choices that might be made according to organisational circumstances are set out below.

Small, privately owned or stock market quoted, growing organisation

Your organisation wants to retain business leaders and other key people, who are crucial to its growth. These people are highly marketable and they know it! In the case of a privately-owned company, a stock market flotation may be considered in a couple of years.

You might consider a two-pronged approach: a cash bonus plan and an Enterprise Management Initiative (EMI). The cash bonus, paid annually, would be linked to key performance indicators comprising lag measures of past performance, such as profits or sales and lead indicators of future performance, for example customer satisfaction. The EMI would enable you to award options over £3m worth of shares in your company. This offers considerable scope in terms of the level of awards and how many people receive them. For example, if your organisation has 100 people, you could award share options worth £100,000 to each of 30 key people. "Key" would be for you to define. Alternatively, you could award £100,000 each to the top 10 business leaders, £50,000 to the next 20 key people and around £14,000 each to everybody else. That could make everybody think like a business leader and take a very close interest in the success of your organisation.

Medium size, stock market quoted organisation

Your organisation wants to kick-start growth which has been sluggish during the last two to three years. Without growth, competitive threats will intensify and business leaders and other key people will feel your organisation has a limited future and, therefore, little opportunity for them. You want to give them the chance to take the business forward and be rewarded for it – but performance must be sustained.

Your first move could be to introduce a cash bonus plan designed to improve short-term performance. Payments would be linked to challenging performance targets covering individual and company performance. The plan would pay-out quarterly (emphasising the importance of performance improvement in the short-term) but 50% of the payment would be "banked" until the next quarter (emphasising the importance of sustained performance improvement).

Your second move could be to introduce an approved company share option scheme for the most senior business leaders. The plan's focus would be value creation in the medium term, measured by lead indicators of performance, such as customer satisfaction, process quality, product development times and employee satisfaction.

Subsidiary of a stock market quoted organisation

Your organisation does not have its "own" shares but many of its competitors are stock market quoted companies, which offer share options to business leaders. You could choose between a cash bonus plan and a phantom share option plan, depending on what you want to achieve and the timescale.

If raising performance in the short term is the priority, a cash bonus plan paying out annually, or quarterly if this is a better fit with the business cycle, would be a good choice because it's relatively easy to implement. However, if the required improvement in performance is likely to take two to three years to achieve, a phantom share plan would probably be a better approach. Of course, if you're looking for performance improvement in the short term and long term, you could have a cash bonus plan and a phantom share option scheme, although the aims and targets for each should be clearly differentiated.

Fairly large, stock market quoted organisation

Your organisation is structured along fairly traditional lines – business divisions and central support functions. Some parts of the organisation are far more successful than others, although rewards for business leaders don't reflect the difference. You want business leaders to drive performance of their own division but also take collective responsibility for the long-term financial success of the entire organisation. You might consider a two-pronged approach: a cash bonus plan and a Long Term Incentive Plan (LTIP).

The cash bonus, paid annually, would be linked to the results of the business division or central support function where the business leader works. Results would be defined in relation to key performance indicators and could include personal objectives based on the business leader's role.

The LTIP would award shares, not share options, when performance targets for the entire organisation have been met – after say three years. Performance, ideally, would be assessed against a comparator group of companies – Total Shareholder Return should be the preferred measure. Business Leaders would be able to invest up to 100% of their annual cash bonus in your organisation's shares ("Deferred Shares" to be held in a Trust for say three years) and at the end of the three years receive Matching Shares, providing a performance condition, for example earnings before tax, had been met.

Key points

- Rewarding financial performance alone isn't good enough: targets should include lead indicators of performance such as customer satisfaction, process quality and employee satisfaction. The mix should take into account organisation, business unit and personal objectives.
- Business leaders should be rewarded for short term business results and long term performance improvement: the two are not mutually exclusive.
- Performance targets should be challenging: targets that are easy to achieve lead to mediocre performance and rewards become "an entitlement". That's bad for business.
- Rewards for business leaders set the tone of rewards for everybody else. So make sure they stand up to the same standards of fairness and consistency that applies to everybody else and that they reflect best practice in corporate governance.[7]
- If your organisation is stock-market quoted, encourage business leaders to build and maintain a significant personal shareholding in it. This should focus minds on what's important to the organisation's success and theirs.
- Remember, investors choose where to invest: so some rewards should depend on the performance relative to a comparator group of companies (the competition).

Part three
Reward Extras

These are other reward practices which help build and retain a culture of "togetherness", a culture in which people really feel they are The Together Company's most important investment. They're the extra, special touches which make The Together Company stand out from the crowd. They are highly visible in people's day-to-day work. They acknowledge excellence, they tap into what people value as individuals and they keep them informed about what matters most and what they can expect to receive in return.

Customised reward strategies

Today's workforce is more diverse that ever before and people's expectations and priorities often change with stages in their life. The resulting desire of employees for greater choice and flexibility over life and work has led an increasing number of organisations to replace one-size-fits-all reward programmes with customised reward packages. Many of these new approaches have been spearheaded by flexible benefits, sometimes called benefits choice, but a wide range of work-life options and working arrangements are now included. Customised reward strategies are viewed increasingly as a competitive differentiator, especially when it comes to attracting and retaining employees.

Recognition and celebration

Clearly recognition and celebration can't replace pay; but rewards that employees value go far, far beyond the financial ones. Just ask employees what makes them stay with the organisation (or leave!). A solid approach to pay and strong supporting recognition go hand-in-hand, and help create a positive, can-do culture, where people feel valued and appreciated. And lots of recognition isn't expensive - the "thank-you", concert ticket or CD. Successful recognition is linked to business strategy and when it's coupled with financial reward, it's a powerful reminder of what matters most.

A rewarding workplace

This is about far more than pay. There are three crucial aspects: the manager-employee relationship; role quality / job satisfaction; and the physical environment. Lots of research has shown that these so-called "intangible rewards" are key drivers of job satisfaction. They are important too, in terms of providing the right support and tools to do the best possible job and to encourage ways of working, for teamworking, that support business success.

Reward communications

Not everybody shares the same view about how they are rewarded. Sometimes employees just don't know how their rewards are determined and what they're eligible for. In addition, most employees have little idea of how much their reward package is worth to them, financially. If they did, many might be pleasantly surprised. That's why reward communications are important. Reward communications should do two things. First, increase employees' awareness of what's being offered and show how much money the organisation invests in employee rewards – overall and on an individual basis. Second, spell out clearly how people will be rewarded and what the organisation expects in return.

CHAPTER TWELVE
Customised reward strategies

At a glance

Over the last few years the range of employee benefits offered by organisations has increased significantly. Many organisations now offer benefits as diverse as pet insurance, reflexology, massage, car wash, crèche, duvet days ("I don't feel like coming to work today"), dental insurance and holiday cottages. Working patterns have changed too – part-time, term-time and home-working options, and sabbaticals or career breaks are increasingly commonplace.

These benefits and working patterns have come about for three key reasons:

- The workforce is more diverse than ever and, over time, people's lifestyle, needs and aspirations change, so the standard, fixed benefits package or the fixed 9 to 5 working day are longer seen as viable by many people and organisations.
- The cost of employee benefits is substantial – typically 25-40% of an organisation's base salary costs – and the cost of some benefits, healthcare in particular, has been rising for several years and is still rising.
- The 24/7 economy – which is partly to do with globalisation and partly to do with changing lifestyles, where people expect to be able to buy products or access services when they want to, not when somebody else says they can.

These changes have had a profound affect on the way The Together Company looks at reward – from the perspective of business requirements and employees' needs. It has responded in two main ways:

- Replacing the one-size-fits all benefits package and fixed hours culture by benefits packages and working options which match the needs of the business, allow employees to choose the ones which suit them best and to change these as their circumstances alter.
- Using cost effective delivery mechanisms, such as HR contact centres and

intranet / internet sites which include practical tools for evaluating various benefits and work-life options.

Not all organisations, of course, have moved at pace to implement these flexible approaches. Some, more than others, need to be totally convinced of the business case before they implement changes. However, there is no doubt in my mind that the days of the one-size-fits all approach to reward are numbered. The age of customised reward strategies has arrived.

Customised benefits packages

While the range of employee benefits offered, who receives them and the cost to the organisation and to employees can differ, sometimes widely, between organisations, customised approaches to employee benefits in The Together Company fall into two categories:

- Flexible benefits
- Voluntary benefits.

Before setting out what these approaches look like, a brief description of the one-size-fits all or so-called "standard benefits package" will put them in context. This is best described as a fixed package of benefits provided for all employees where the organisation pays for all the benefits and there's no benefits choice on offer. Levels of benefit may vary by employee group, for example free private medical insurance may be provided only to managers or by length of employment, for example an additional 1 day's holiday is given after 5 or 10 years with the company. These days the package may include some of the "newer" benefits such as dental insurance, critical illness insurance and gym membership. Now back to customised approaches.

Flexible benefits

The term "flexible benefits" covers a wide variety of plans, from simple "cash or car" options to plans in which the employee can choose from a menu of benefits within a set budget. Flexible benefits have become increasingly popular in the last five years as organisations have competed for scarce talent in an ever more diverse employment market and as technology has advanced, making it relatively easy and cost effective to identify good applications supporting their administration. Key features of a typical flexible benefits plan in The Together Company are as follows:

- Employees can vary the level of a selected benefit. Take life assurance, for example. The employee could choose cover of two, three or four times their salary.
- Employees can change their choices. This is usually allowed on an annual basis but sometimes more frequently, subject to any longer term contractual commitments into which the organisation has had to enter, for example in relation to cars.
- Many companies insist that employees retain certain core benefits, such as, a minimum level of holiday, life assurance cover and accident insurance.

There is virtually no limit to the choice of potential benefits for inclusion in a flexible benefits plan. Just like a successful restaurant changes its menu to reflect the seasons of the year and retain loyal diners, the flexible benefits menu needs to change to reflect employees' needs and aspirations. Figure 12.1 shows the make-up of flexible plans reported in some recent research[1]. The numbers refer to the percentage of organisations which include the benefit.

FIGURE 12.1   Flexible benefits: Top 20 Benefits

Childcare vouchers	81	Pension: money purchase	41
Private medical insurance	68	Travel insurance	39
Buy/sell some annual holidays	66	Hospital/healthcare cash plan	39
Life assurance for employee	64	Leisure/retail vouchers	38
Dental insurance	58	Give-as-you-earn/payroll giving	37
Critical illness for employee	54	Health screening for partners	35
Health screening for employee	48	Company cars	34
Pension: additional voluntary contributions	47	Alternative to cars (cash, hire, etc)	34
Personal accident insurance for employee	46	Group income protection	33
Critical illness for partners of employees	42	Pension: final salary	32

What are the advantages of flexible benefits? According to the same piece of research, the top three advantages, in the eyes of organisations that have introduced them, are:

- Recognises the diverse needs and values of the workforce (80%)
- Improves image of employer (61%)
- Promotes employee understanding/appreciation of benefits (59%)

Interestingly, a reduction in benefits costs does not feature here – remember, rising costs was one of the drivers for change. I suspect that cost reduction has been harder to achieve than many organisations thought when they set off down the flexible benefits route. In fact, anecdotal evidence from my consulting experience suggests "cost-neutral" is the most likely outcome.

Complexity of administration, costs of implementation/administration and getting approval for the business case are the top three problems associated with flexible benefits plans. But, as more organisations believe flexible benefits help tackle diversity issues, the pressure will mount for simpler, more cost-effective administration. That, over time, will help organisations build the business case.

Voluntary benefits

Voluntary benefits are a half-way house between the standard, fixed package of benefits and flexible benefits. Employees can have access to a range of products and services on which their employer has negotiated a discount with suppliers, but the employee pays for the benefit. This is David Lloyd Leisure's approach (see case study in Chapter 1, The Together Company) where employees have access to a wide range of benefits with discounts negotiated by the parent company, Whitbread.

In a voluntary benefits plan employees in The Together Company can log-on to a website or look through a catalogue and buy as much, or as little, as they want. Providers may offer anything from mortgages, conveyancing and healthcare plans to shopping discounts, wine clubs and designer clothes. Figure 12.2 shows the 20 benefits most frequently included in a voluntary plan[2]. The numbers refer to the percentage of organisations which include the benefit.

FIGURE 12.2   Voluntary Benefits: Top 20 benefits

Additional voluntary contributions to defined benefit/money purchase pension	66	Employer's own products or services	46
		Legal advice/helpline	40
Group personal pension	63	Retail products (e.g. electrical goods, CDs)	40
Healthcare/hospital cash plan	59	Travel insurance	39
Private medical insurance	58	Optical care/vouchers (above statutory)	39
Gym membership	57	Debt counselling/helpline	37
Childcare vouchers	54	Health screening	36
Stakeholder pension	52	Dental insurance	36
Life assurance	49	Inland Revenue-approved save-as-you-earn (SAYE) sharesave plan	35
Season ticket loan	47		
Leisure/entertainment services (e.g. theatre tickets or travel packages	47	Personal accident insurance	35

The appeal of voluntary benefits to The Together Company is that they are ready-made, easy to implement and cheap to administer. They are viewed as part of the overall reward package (no longer are they the poor person's answer to benefits) and products offered can be cheaper than on the high street, although some internet deals may be hard to beat. My top tips to help keep employees happy are:

- Communicate the quality of the voluntary benefits not just the savings
- Ensure products and services are supplied by reputable providers
- Monitor what's being purchased
- If the plan is outsourced to a third party make sure there is a policy for resolving any disputes over what's provided – and get information on the outcome of any disputes
- Review the contents of the plan regularly to ensure it reflects employees' needs and preferences.

Organisations which are unsure of the business case for implementing a fully flexible benefits plan, sometimes choose voluntary benefits. This enables them to keep their options open by, either moving to a fully flexible benefits plan at a later date when take-up of voluntary benefits and potential costs and advantages can be quantified, or expanding the range of benefits offered by a voluntary plan.

Flexible working arrangements[3]

Do any of the following sound familiar?

- Long hours at the office
- Traffic jams on the way to work
- Eating lunch at your desk or or not breaking for lunch at all
- Taking work home in the evening and at the weekends.

All are reasons why many people long for a better work-life balance. By offering flexible working arrangements The Together Company sends an important message: "Healthy employees, with a good balance between work and home life, are "good for business".

But what do I mean by good for business? This includes helping to recruit and retain employees and meeting their needs and those of customers, and reducing absenteeism. When responsibility for rostering is handed over from the manager to employees, for example, employees are often more easily able to swop shifts / work times when necessary.

We are used to accessing services around-the-clock, but the most commonly reported constraint on implementing flexible working practices is operational pressures, for example having enough employees in the right place at the right time to satisfy business needs. Not only that, concerns about line managers' attitude to flexible working and their ability to manage employees working more flexibly often emerge as major constraints. In my experience, employee resistance or lack of interest is rarely a problem, although some employees are concerned that their career opportunities may be adversely affected.

The support of business leaders is crucial to making flexibility work. But, alone, they can't be expected to fly the flexibility flag. In The Together Company, everybody sees the potential benefits of working flexibly, for the organisation and themselves. They demonstrate this belief in lots of ways, such as putting forward the business case to work from home once-a-month or requesting a secondment to another part of the organisation or to a different organisation, to bring new ideas into their organisation.

Tensions will always exist between organisational policies which are presented as "flexible" and "work-life balance friendly" and a workplace culture where, for example people are expected to work long hours without any compensating time-off or where e-mails fly around the office at 5pm and managers "demand" a reply before people finish work for the day. Actions speak louder than words!

Flexible working choices

So, what's on offer and which ones work best? Figure 12.3 shows a summary of what's on offer in many organisations today.[3] This isn't an exhaustive list but it gives an indication of the kind of practices which your organisation might want to consider introducing. In reality, of course, it's unlikely that employees can pick and choose exactly what they like from such a list; you will have to decide which employees are able to work flexibly in the light of the nature of the work they do and the business requirements.

FIGURE 12.3   Flexible working choices

Flexi-time
Compressed working week (e.g. 4 day week)
Part-time
Term-time working
Job share
Home-working on a regular basis
Annualised hours
Secondments to another organisation
Career breaks / sabbaticals
Time off to work in the community

Around a quarter of employees are estimated to make use of flexible working and the numbers have been rising at a rate of 20% over the last three years. Part-time working is by far the most popular. As far as "which practices work best" is concerned, the answer is "all of them, in the right place and at the right time". Together Companies focus on getting two things right:

- Practices which appeal to all employees. That doesn't mean all practices appeal to everybody all of the time. The Together Company gives employees different options which take operational constraints into account and agrees with them the flexible working practices which are likely to work best for both of them. It also carries out some employee research and talks to organisations that have tried and tested different flexible working practices. This can be worth its weight in gold. However, a few words of caution: just because it's worked in another organisation doesn't mean that it's right for yours.
- Ensuring the quality of support services, such as workplace crèches, medical centres and allowances, such as childcare vouchers or assistance towards the care of dependent relatives, is high.

Contrary to opinion in some quarters, flexible working and work-life balance practices aren't appropriate and affordable only in large organisations, as Bacharach Europe Ltd, winner of Employee Benefits Awards 2006 – Work Life Balance Policy shows (Figure 12.4).

FIGURE 12.4   Bacharach Europe Ltd – Work Life Balance Policy[4]

Bacharach Europe is a small business with 90 employees based in Warwickshire, supplying and manufacturing gas detection equipment. Its work-life balance initiative has been placed at the heart of company culture in a bid to aid employee retention. Employees' needs are accommodated as much as possible. A reflection of this success is an employee absence rate of around two days per employee per year. Requests for flexible working arrangements are actively considered, with a number of employees working term-time and school hours or job share arrangements. All employees are entitled to time off to give blood or donate bone marrow. Bacharach also pays for any training employees undertake in their own time. Independent pension advisors are provided during working hours and a discounted will-writing service is made available. Fresh fruit and subsidised healthy lunches, free tea and coffee machines and water fountains are provided for all employees. Bacharach organises "Just 4 Fun" events for employees and their families and encourage employees to take part in charity fund raising challenges. Each month it awards the workplace team which has "gone the extra mile" a GEM Award, a personalised cake and £300 to spend on any equipment that will make their lives easier. What made this entry so outstanding in the judges' eyes was that this is not an organisation with huge resources and large profits, just a company which has set a target of being an "employer of choice" and in order to achieve this has decided to offer employees everything that's feasibly possible.

Resolving the three flexible working problems

Three common problems account for most of the constraints surrounding the implementation of flexible working. Here are some practical tips for resolving them.

Problem 1: Demonstrating fairness between different employees

The top problem for managers is demonstrating fairness between different employees (or groups of employees) when dealing with requests to work flexibly. Actions to help here are:

- Enabling all employees to request (not be entitled to) flexible working rather than just parents with young children, or carers of adults, as required by UK legislation, is a good first step. This should help everybody see that their requests are being considered on the same basis.
- Having a transparent process which takes into account three key factors:
  - Employees' skills and preferences
  - Type of work, for example how much time is spent away from "the office"
  - Team needs.
- Self-rostering – when the work roster for a team is devised by team members rather than the team leader, employees are usually better able to recognise the importance of balancing business and their individual needs.

Problem 2: Line managers' inability to manage effectively flexible employees

The second problem is that line managers' express concern about their ability to manage groups of employees working flexibly. Their concerns tend to focus on an inability to manage workflow, managing the performance of their team (output rather than "presenteeism") and communicating with the team. Actions to consider here include:

- Give managers coaching / feedback – from the HR department and a senior manager / business leader
- Provide information about legal requirements – a summary of the key points for example
- Give written guidance and advice about your organisation's policy on flexible working – again key points plus the advantages for the organisation, for employees and points to watch, for example, making sure business requirements

are met
- Provide guidance and examples of where flexible working has operated successfully in the organisation, on your organisation's intranet.

Problem 3: Employees feel their career prospects will suffer

Some employees may be reluctant to request flexible working because they feel that not being "present" full time (that is, there're not "seen") will mean they lose out on career and promotion prospects. Three actions to allay their concerns are:

- Ensure training and career development opportunities are available to employees working flexibly and monitor take-up rates among different flexibly working groups of employees
- Improve communication of the flexible working arrangements available – using both paper and electronic channels (Chapter 15, Reward communications)
- Include questions about flexible working in employee opinion / satisfaction / engagement surveys – this could be done in an annual survey or through a "pulse survey" which taps into different departments every six months.

Four steps to a customised reward strategy

It's tempting, of course, to consider flexible benefits, voluntary benefits or flexible working if the market place competition has done so, or is planning to do so. But, irrespective of what the competition is up to, it's crucial that your organisation gets value for money from its investment in employee benefits and working arrangements whatever its strategy. The Together Company's strategy is based on sound research which builds the business case. By following four steps you too can implement a customised reward strategy that delivers value for your organisation and for employees.

Step 1: Defining your objectives

What do you want your employee benefits package to do? What advantages would more flexible working offer? Typical objectives could be to:

- Attract and retain more talented people
- Improve retention among key employee groups for example, customer-facing teams
- Increase your employment offer to acceptance ratio

- Improve customer service at high sales times, for example lunchtime for a retail store
- Provide better cover for absence and holidays, or
- Reduce absenteeism.

Step 2: Evaluating your current approach

This has three parts:

1. What benefits and working arrangements do you offer and how do they compare with the competition?

If you've not looked at this in the last three years, you could find benefits packages in particular have changed significantly. You need to review the costs of benefits too. Again, if you haven't monitored this regularly, you could be in for some nasty surprises. Any differences in benefits provision by employee group, for example managers receive a higher level of medical insurance, should be either supported by market data or reflect your organisation's culture. Existing arrangements will, in part, define your culture, but, if you want to change the culture, from hierarchical to single status or from highly structured to flexible for example, you need to identify which benefits approach and flexible working options will best help achieve the desired culture – and the required business results.

2. How do employees feel about your current approach and what new benefits or flexible working options might they be interested in?

A simple survey is all that is required here. It provides The Together Company with information about:

- The value employees attach to the benefits package – financially and emotionally
- Which benefits they particularly like or dislike
- The degree to which they would be prepared to contribute to part of the cost of new benefits that interest them
- The demand for flexible working
- Practical ideas about the sort of flexibility which would work well in their department.

This type of research pays big dividends when you're developing a new approach (Step 3) and when you're communicating it to employees (Step 4).

3. What employment law and IT issues do you need to consider?

How will employment contracts be affected by flexible working or benefits changes, especially flexible benefits? Can your current HR and IT systems cope with flexible benefits or voluntary benefits or do you need to outsource administration and, if so, at what cost? These questions need well-researched answers because without them, it will be difficult to build a sound business case. Not only that, you may not be able to meet employees' expectations which have emerged from your employee research and lack of cost data could put back your timetable for change, or at worst, jeopardise your entire strategy.

Step 3: Developing your new approach

The findings from your work in Steps 1 and 2 should highlight things you are doing well and areas where change is required, and the expected business benefits. This will point to potential options for the future.

The results of your market research about what the competition is doing (criteria for assessing the competitiveness of your benefits is given in Chapter 6, Understanding your employment market) should identify which additional benefits or flexible working practices will differentiate your organisation from the competition and raise their perceived value among employees. If the results suggest that a wider range of benefits is needed to meet the objectives you set in Step 1, the choice would be between the following three main approaches:

- Introduce a voluntary benefits plan
- Introduce a flexible benefits plan
- Enhance the current standard benefits package.

While you might be convinced that flexible benefits, for example, is the route to follow, costs and IT / HR systems limitations may prevent you from doing so this year. But if attraction and retention are key issues for you, introducing a low-cost, high value voluntary benefits plan this year, followed by flexible benefits in two years time, could be the best strategy.

If your objectives for a customised reward strategy, your external market research and employees' views suggest that there is a good business case for flexible working, remember that, like benefits, there is no off-the-shelf approach which can be implemented immediately. The Together Company introduces flexible working in a measured way rather than "going for broke". It starts with the most popular choices identified in your employee research and where the business benefits are likely to materialise most quickly.

Step 4: Communicating your new approach

Three key questions need to be answered here:

- How will your customised reward strategy be launched – all at once or phased, and how?
- What internal brand will reinforce your employee value proposition?
- What's the best way to encourage take-up of the new features - flexible benefits, voluntary benefits and flexible working?

Communicating your new customised reward strategy should not be a one-off event. After the initial publicity, you need to keep reinforcing the key messages and tap into employees' take-up of flexible working for example, or voluntary benefits. This will enable you to adapt the strategy, as employees' needs and preferences change. Ideas about how to communicate and put together a communications plan are set out in Chapter 15, Reward communications.

Is it right for you?

Customised reward strategies can be competitive differentiators for different types and sizes of organisation. Some of the choices that might be made according to circumstances are summarised below.

Small but growing organisation

If your organisation is to achieve its plans for growth, you must attract and retain talented people, while keeping benefits costs under tight control. The simplest approach would be to provide a standard benefits package for all employees, which included (say) the following:
- 20-23 days holiday
- A money purchase pension plan (company contribution and employee contribution both at 3%; if the employee makes a higher contribution, this could be matched by you)
- Life assurance of 1-2 times salary
- Limited flexibility over benefits, for example, exchanging a good attendance bonus for extra days' holiday or "buying" extra life assurance
- Some flexibility to work from home on a few occasions.

It might be worth investigating voluntary benefits, as these could be attractive in terms of minimal cost to your organisation and additional benefits for employees.

Fairly large organisation

Your organisation has had a standard benefits package for many years but you feel it has fallen behind the competition and employee opinion data suggest the package isn't particularly attractive. You could consider an approach along the following lines:
- Retain the standard benefits package but offer enhancements which are cost effective for the organisation and employees. Benefits could include:
  - 23-25 days holiday
  - Final salary pension scheme remains open to existing employees only; a money purchase plan for all new starters (company contribution and employee contribution both at 5%; if the employee makes a higher contribution, this could be matched by you)
  - Life assurance of 3-4 times salary
  - Private healthcare (usually provided for managers, but increasingly for all employees)
- Introduce a voluntary benefits plan so employees can choose additional benefits that suit their lifestyle
- Provide a comprehensive range of flexible working patterns, such as part-time, term time, home-working and flexitime
- Consider introducing a flexible benefits plan in say two years, once the impact of voluntary benefits on recruitment, retention and employee satisfaction is known.

High tech / professional services organisation

Your organisation competes for talented, knowledge based people who are in short supply. At the moment you offer a standard benefits package for all employees. You are keen to retain a single status culture, so your approach might be along the following lines:
- A benefits package which includes the following standard benefits:
  - 25 days holiday
  - A money purchase plan (company contribution and employee contribution both at 5%; if the employee makes a higher contribution, this could be matched by you)
  - Life assurance of 3-4 times salary
  - Laptop computers
- A voluntary benefits plan, so employees can choose additional benefits that suit their lifestyle; or a flexible benefits plan which offers a wide range of benefits.

- A comprehensive range of flexible working patterns, such as part-time, term time, home-working and flexitime. These might include IT / telephone connections for home-based working.

Key points

- The days of the standard fixed benefits package and 9 to 5 working day with no choice or flexibility, are gone forever – benefits choice and different ways of working are here to stay.
- Flexible or voluntary benefits enable employees to customise their rewards to their life stages rather than have to take what's deemed to be appropriate for their age or years of employment.
- Don't assume employees know what's on offer: communicate, communicate and communicate.
- Employees' interests and requirements change with circumstances, so it's important to monitor the take-up rates of individual benefits within flexible and voluntary plans and modify the packages accordingly.
- Assess the effectiveness of flexible working options too. What benefits have they brought to the business and to employees? Measure the results against the objectives you set out to achieve, such as improve retention of key people, reduce absenteeism or increase customer satisfaction at busy trading times.
- When you've done that, look for linkages between the achievement of these objectives and profit. That's the way to a winning customised reward strategy.

CHAPTER THIRTEEN
Recognition and celebration

Case study

Recognition for "going the extra mile" at T.G.I. Friday's

T.G.I. Friday's is one of the most recognisable restaurant brands in the UK. The look is flamboyant; the atmosphere fun and buzzing. T.G.I. Friday's guiding philosophy is: "By treating our guests as if they were our friends, invited to our homes and thinking about their needs and expectations, our guests become loyal. Thinking also about their changing tastes, comfort and enjoyment ensures they have a good experience, all the time, every time".

Each of the 45 T.G.I. Friday's restaurants (called stores) in the UK employs a wide range of people – waiters / waitresses, chefs, bartenders, hosts, server assistants, kitchen porters and administrators. These "team members" are led by a General Manager and Management Team. 43% of the 3,000 people working at T.G.I. Friday's are under 22 years of age. Employee turnover in the stores is 18%; that's well below the average for the hospitality sector.

So, how does T.G.I. Friday's create a work environment that's valued by team members and makes them want to stay with the company? The answer is "in lots of ways", such as recruiting team members for their attitude towards teamwork, in addition to their traditional restaurant skills, providing extensive training in all aspects of the business and encouraging new ideas and innovations. All of this is underpinned by the company's five values: balance (guests, team members and company); integrity; excellence; recognition and enjoyment. These values guide everybody personally on how they behave and the way they do business, and are reinforced by Whitbread's guiding principles of "belief in people and teamwork, continuous improvement, passion for winning and caring for guests".

One of these values, recognition, is lived in a highly visible way. T.G.I. Friday's believes that a good job should never go unnoticed. When the company sees team members going that extra mile for a guest or colleagues, or working really hard to pass accredited certifications and achieve new skills and knowledge, they award a "recognition pin". There are around 100 recognition pins that can be awarded for all sorts of achievements. Figure 13.1 shows some of the pin badges that can be awarded, what they're awarded for and who are allowed to award them.

FIGURE 13.1	Examples of Recognition Pins at T.G.I. Friday's	
	What the award is for	*Who can give the award*
WOW	Wow, guest compliment, moment of truth	Any manager
WTT (Walk the Talk)	For displaying one of the 5 star values	Any manager
WTT star	Consistently displaying all 5 values to guests and team members	General / Operations Manager
Step Change	For living a change in behaviour / implementing a new initiative for our guests	Operations Manager
Twinning Pin	For recognition for initiatives with the "twin" store in the U.S.	Operations Manager
Store Pin	For outstanding commitment to your store	Any manager
£1,000	Achieving £1,000 personal sales in one shift	Any manager
Mystery Diner	Part of the team responsible for a 100% mystery diner score	General Manager
Great Ideas	To recognise a Manager or Team Member who has forwarded a great idea that benefits either the guest, other team members or the Company / store	Any manager
MVP pin	Being "Most Valuable Player"	General Manager
Friday's UK	Commitment to the success of the company	General Manager
Whitbread Pin	Outstanding commitment and passion to Whitbread	Operations Manager / Directors
Bronze Star	Ongoing praiseworthy performance	General Manager / Operations Manager
Silver Star	Outstanding commitment, success and passion	Operations Manager
Gold Star	Excellence in job role, commitment to company	Directors
Walk the Talk Gold Star	Outstanding and on-going commitment to the 4 steps of Walk the Talk, supporting management and company achieving vision and mission, living the 5 star values and instilling then into other team members at all times. The highest recognition awarded in the UK.	Awarded by Executive Team member

Team members can be nominated for recognition by a colleague, a manager, or a guest or recognised directly by the head office and Executive teams.

There are recognition pins for completing training too. These include pins for first aid, fire and general health and safety, participating in the training team at a new store opening and an "A Team" pin for completing 5 new store openings. Certification pins are awarded for accredited job skills such as door host, administrator, bartender, master bartender, server assistant, store person and manager. Length of service pins are given at 1, 5 and 10 years employment.

"People love pin badges", says Ruth Hutchison, the HR Director of T.G.I. Friday's. "They wear them with pride, on their braces and hats. The motivational power is in the symbolism – who receives it, who gives it and when it's given. Recognition pins are part of our culture and a very visible way of showing to team members and our guests, what T.G.I. Friday's values most".

Recognition and celebration
At a glance

Of course money matters. Few of us come to work purely for the love of it. But there's something else that matters a lot too. It's called "recognition", especially the non-financial kind. When it happens, people feel wanted and valued – that's The Together Company. When it doesn't happen, people feel disheartened and unappreciated, and when that happens it's bad for business.

Recognition and celebration in The Together Company isn't reserved for those "special achievements". On a day-to-day basis, it's often the "little things" that count. Just knowing peoples names, remembering their birthdays and anniversaries, and celebrating their achievements, matters a lot to people. We are individuals, with our own likes, dislikes and personality (apologies to the personality profilers) and we don't always want to be recognised in one, standard way that happens in many organisations. One of our hospitality clients asks all new employees to write down their favourite things – sport, music, food, drink, hobby, travel and books. Recognition awards are tailored to what the individual employee values most.

One of the big advantages of recognition is that it's appropriate for Together Companies of all sizes, from a few employees to tens of thousands of people and it can work successfully in all types of businesses – private, quoted, public and voluntary. Pay practices supported by recognition and celebration are powerful communicators of what matters to The Together Company – its business priorities, corporate values and, critically, the behaviours necessary to deliver results for customers and shareholders.

Six steps to successful recognition

By following six key steps, you too can create a culture where recognition and celebration are part of the way your organisation does business.

Step 1: Focusing on the things that matter most

Make recognition depend on what you need employees to do. This is where alignment with business strategy comes in. Too often, the criteria for recognition are unclear. If teamwork, customer service and innovation are business priorities, make these the focus of recognition. When cost reduction is a priority, be specific – translate it into things people can do, individually or in their team, to save money. If you want employees to "go the extra mile" give examples which they can relate to, such as voluntarily helping colleagues in other departments at exceptionally busy times, arranging a special delivery to a customer's home at a time that suits them, or getting involved in community projects or charities that your organisation supports.

Does your organisation recognise the things that matter most? Find out by doing the exercise below:

1. Write a list of your organisation's business objectives
2. Write a list of the things employees are actually recognised for
3. Ask yourself the question: "How well do my two lists match?" If the answer is: "Very well", you recognise employees for the things that matter most to business success. If the answer is: "Very poorly", then either you recognise lots of things that don't matter to business success or, you don't recognise employees' achievements at all.

Being crystal clear about what matters to your organisation's success will set you off on the right track.

Step 2: Targeting the right people

This may sound obvious, but far too many recognition programmes try to appeal to everybody and after the initial publicity hype, lose their appeal. One of the reasons why employee-of-the-month programmes for example, are successful in many organisations is that they recognise only twelve people a year. They highlight the best individual achievements. Manchester United's VVIP scheme is shown in Figure 13.2.

FIGURE 13.2 Manchester United: VVIP Employees of the Month Scheme

---

The VVIP Employees of the Month Scheme has been running since September 2004 and through this scheme 73 members of staff have been recognised for "living the UNITED values". Officially VVIP means "Vision and Values in Practice", but it also means "Very, Very Important Person". As a result the 73 employees were invited to attend, as VIP guests of the Directors, a Premier League home game - dining in the VIP Suite and watching the game from the Directors' Box. Also, those nominated but not chosen are informed and, in recognition, have been invited to attend special events, for example, the Northern Film Premiere of Ocean's Twelve at the Red Cinema. Also, a prestigious trophy award is made to the Employee of the Season at the Company Christmas Party and repeated on the pitch at the first home game in January, in front of a capacity crowd of 76,000 and shown live on Sky!

Some examples of VVIP are below:

- Excelling during a recent visit by our newest sponsor, Air Asia, to launch their sponsorship. Worked extremely long hours before and after the visit, including late nights and weekends.
- Covered extensively during sickness absence in the department and worked at great personal inconvenience. Cut short lunch times, arrived early, stayed late to ensure shift changes went smoothly.
- Kitchen porter has got to be the worst job! But while others around him moan, he lifts the spirit of everybody around him, organises them when they're short of people and keeps smiling.

If getting people to work together more effectively is a priority, identify the areas of your business where teamwork matters most, both within teams and between teams.

The Together Company makes sure that everybody in the team can win, not just team leaders, managers or the extrovert members of the team. And it doesn't forget project teams or groups set up to solve specific problems; they receive recognition too. Organisational success of course, is a result of the collective efforts and contribution made by all employees, so there may be times when your organisation wants to celebrate organisational success by recognising everybody.

So, target the right people carefully. A recognition programme that includes groups of people solely on the grounds "if we don't include them, they'll feel discriminated against, left out or disgruntled", is doomed to failure.

Step 3: Making it personal

Not everybody likes the same things, so The Together Company ensures that recognition and celebration follow suit. Giving everybody a bottle of champagne or theatre tickets is fine if you know they like champagne or going to the theatre. But if they don't, its motivational impact is likely to be, at best, neutral and at worst, negative. It's a waste of money too. There's no substitute for conducting some employee research to find out what people value and the research doesn't have to be onerous or time consuming. A few focus groups can reap dividends and provide a wealth of information about what employees like and how they like to be recognised. Some employees feel embarrassed when their photograph is displayed in the main reception, while others like being in the limelight.

There are lots of different types of recognition – verbal, written, work-related, financial or symbolic.[1] Try something spontaneous, for example give managers a pot of money each month and let them make on-the-spot awards for special achievements. Experiment from traditional gifts to approaches that challenge the limits of your company's style. Figure 13.3 gives some examples of recognition which doesn't cost a fortune.

If you want to "push the boat out" and you don't mind spending a few hundred pounds, then think about doing something that's really different from conventional recognition. One of the most interesting examples I've come across was the way the Managing Director of a European tour operator recognised everybody's contribution

---

FIGURE 13.3 Low-cost, high value recognition

- Personal "thank you" note or letter
- Personal "pat-on-the-back"
- Certificate or plaque that records the employee's achievement
- Acknowledge the employee's achievement at a team meeting
- Publicise achievements in company magazine or newsletter
- Nominate somebody for a formal recognition programme
- Training opportunity to attend a conference / event
- Opportunity for visibility by making presentation at meetings
- Provide interesting work or project or stretch assignment
- Learning opportunity – develop a new skill, cross training

---

to better than expected half-yearly profits, achieved ahead of schedule. The MD asked the HR Team to spend half the night decorating the head office with balloons, so that when employees (and customers) walked in the next morning, they knew something special had happened. The MD also sent a personally addressed e-mail thanking everybody.

Step 4: Making it timely

Immediacy counts! Receiving recognition long after the excitement of "winning" has passed is hardly going to make employees wax lyrical about recognition. It has the maximum impact shortly after the achievement. Admittedly, this is not always possible, but giving feedback quickly by, for example, letting people know they've won an award or have been short-listed for a top award, is simple to do and keeps recognition alive.

When people's achievements aren't noticeable immediately, for example in research and development environments where the time from product concept to commercial launch can be several months and sometimes several years, recognising and celebrating milestones along the way tells employees their continuing contribution is valued. The Together Company applies this principle to project work too, where some team members may be part-time, and it recognises their contribution not just when they leave the team but when the project's completed.

Step 5: Recognising the unsung heroes

Don't forget those who nominate and recognise their work colleagues – managers, team members and employees in other parts of your organisation. They need recognition too. They are the unsung heroes of recognition schemes who work tirelessly to get people involved and get as much personal satisfaction from their actions as the people who get the recognition. Tell them in person, tell others by e-mail and emphasise at team meetings the importance of showing appreciation.

Step 6: Measuring the results

As a minimum, The Together Company measures how recognition affects employee satisfaction scores and employee retention rates. This is done through either an annual or more frequent "pulse surveys". Then it looks for relationships between these employee indicators and business indicators, such as customer satisfaction, cost reduction and profit / revenue growth per employee. This information is a powerful reminder of why recognition matters. Without it, there's little chance of getting management's attention about recognition. Even if you're looking to introduce a recognition scheme for the first time, and don't have this data in-house, have a look at what other organisations have done and how they've benefited.

Resolving the four recognition problems

Four common problems account for most of the reasons why recognition programmes either fail completely or have a lacklustre performance. Here are some practical tips for resolving them.

Problem 1: Little use of recognition

The first recognition problem is lack of use. This happens when employees lose interest because nobody ever seems to be recognised. If this has happened in your organisation, you need to do three things:

- Find out the number of people who have been recognised and which departments feature more than others
- Find out what employees know about recognition – its purpose, the criteria and the rewards
- Make sure your written material gets employees' attention. Does yours excite anybody? Tell employees what's expected and share stories about the results achieved by different parts of your organisation working closely together. Simply communicating the recognition programme may raise employees' awareness significantly and lead to someone coming up with the best business improvement idea this year.

Problem 2: Undervalued by employees

The second recognition problem is that employees simply don't attach any value to recognition. Why do they feel this way? Sometimes it's because managers simply don't believe in recognition. For them, reward is just about money. Sometimes it's to do with the way recognition is given. If recognition comes over in a patronising way or as a "second thought", employees are bound to feel undervalued. To make matters worse, employees who haven't been recognised usually feel this way too, because that's what they've heard about recognition. The answer to this problem is to do some employee research. Here are three suggestions:

- Run a few focus groups to find out how people feel about recognition (or the lack of it) and what they would change
- Ask people at team meetings for their views
- Ask relative newcomers for their "first impressions".

Then get on and change employees' negative perceptions to positive ones.

Problem 3: Lack of credibility

Lack of credibility is the third recognition problem. Employees simply feel that the reasons people are recognised don't match the published criteria. In other words, there's favouritism. This problem is really about trust. Schemes that have been around for several years sometimes acquire their own "unwritten rules", for example the business division with the largest number of employees gets most recognition awards. Actions to improve credibility include:

- Outlaw any "unwritten rules" – top management must take the lead here and show that it really cares about recognition by getting involved personally in award presentations, for example
- Communicate recognition criteria and awards widely, so there's complete transparency about what's expected and why certain individuals or teams have been recognised
- Involve employees in decisions about who should receive recognition. If teams are eligible, consider letting team members decide who, if anybody, should receive individual recognition for special contribution to the team's success.

Problem 4: Perceived inequities

The final recognition problem is perceived inequities. Consider the following scenario. A customer service team in your organisation has been voted "Team of the Year" for delivering great service to key customers. This has been hugely instrumental in raising the profitability of these accounts and in attracting new customers. When the recognition awards are announced, each customer service advisor receives a thank you letter, signed by the divisional director and a £50 gift voucher. However, the team manager receives an all-expenses paid weekend away for two people, at a four-star hotel. How do you think the customer service advisors feel? This example may sound a little far fetched but I've seen it happen many times. Ensure recognition is fair. Otherwise, don't be surprised by a lack of gratitude!

Is it right for you?

The best recognition and celebration matches the organisation's culture, business priorities and its size. However, a personal "pat-on-the-back" or "thank you" note or letter should feature in every organisation. In fact, good relationships with team leaders or business leaders is one of the top job satisfiers and ultimately retentive factors. Here are some other suggestions for recognition and celebration in different types of organisations.

Small but growing organisation

Most people in your organisation know everybody else and they know that only by working together, rather than pursuing their personal agenda, will the organisation succeed. This could be recognised in three simple ways:

- Give retail or leisure vouchers for an outstanding example of teamwork. Employees could have a say in which team won. The team might decide to celebrate together, at a place of their choosing.
- A company event to celebrate everybody's contribution to winning a prestigious customer
- A training opportunity for an individual to attend a conference / event.

Fairly large organisation

Your organisation is organised along fairly traditional lines, with business units, departments and teams. There is a mixture of individual and team based work. Recognition hasn't been a strong point of the organisation's culture, although a few managers are very good at it. You could adopt a three-pronged approach:

- Give managers a sum of money per month to recognise individual examples of going the extra mile, such as customer service, teamwork or being flexible over hours worked. Alternatively, managers could give time-off.
- Introduce a formal recognition programme for example, Employee of the Month, where employees receive a cash sum and a certificate or plaque that records their achievements. Employees should have a significant input to the decision about who receives the award. You might also consider other formal recognition programmes which are linked to specific business objectives, such as improved business processes, cost savings and new product or service ideas.
- Encourage departments or teams to celebrate their own achievements, with funds provided by managers.

Project team-based organisation

Your organisation is based around teams, so recognising the special contribution made by a team (and perhaps particular individual contributions to the team's success) would be a good place to start. The recognition should be tailored to what type of recognition team members' value, for example financial or non-financial. Teams might compete (constructively, I might add) for Team of the Quarter or Team of the Year, based on well-publicised criteria, such as customer satisfaction / service, sales, teamwork or cost saving ideas that worked. Team success should be publicised to encourage even more team success – that shows that your organisation really is committed to teamwork.

High-tech / professional services organisation

Your organisation needs to encourage new ideas and come up with products and services that give it a competitive advantage. So, a key focus for recognition could be breakthrough innovations, unplanned contributions and exceeding performance expectations or project objectives. Awards could be made to individuals or teams and include a conference visit, a special assignment, access to gurus in your field of technology and expense-paid trips.

By publicising achievements in your organisation's magazine or employee newsletter and on the intranet, you convey to employees (and, importantly, customers too) "you are recognised for what matters most". This alone, may encourage other employees to go the extra mile.

Key points

- Recognition should be a positive reward experience and make employees feel special. Sometimes it should be fun!
- Make recognition depend on what you need employees to do. This is where alignment with business strategy comes in.
- Too many recognition programmes try to appeal to everybody – target the right groups of employees.
- Recognition should reflect what people really value. So mix and match financial and non-monetary recognition, but don't assume you know what's best. Ask employees!
- Make sure your written material gets employees' attention. Does yours excite anybody?
- Try something spontaneous, for example give managers a pot of money each month and let them make on-the-spot awards for special achievements.
- Measure the impact of recognition – you need to know if it's living up to employees' expectations and helping achieve what matters most to the business.

CHAPTER FOURTEEN
A rewarding workplace

At a glance

What drives job satisfaction? What motivates people at work? Questions like these have been the basis of many research studies about employee engagement.[1] Additionally, in the last five years, a lot has been written about "best companies to work for" and many organisations want to be one. Being named as a Sunday Times 100 Best Companies to Work For may help them attract the talented people they need.

Why do employees choose one organisation over another? What makes a "Best Company"? Innovative, tangible rewards usually grab the headlines: holiday cottages, days out sailing, relaxation therapies, free strawberries at Wimbledon, 15% bonus for mothers returning to work and renting out a cinema to watch the latest Harry Potter film. But these aren't sufficient to attract and retain talented people. In addition to tangible rewards, talented people look for a workplace which provides intangible "soft" rewards, such as job interest, challenge, social interaction and opportunities to develop. A pleasant working space is part of the equation too.

While a comprehensive analysis of this topic is well outside the scope of this book, an exploration of three critical aspects which make The Together Company a "rewarding workplace" is merited. These aspects are:

- The manager-employee relationship
- Role quality / job satisfaction
- Physical environment.

The manager-employee relationship

Time and time again, employees tell me that while competitive pay and benefits are important, some of the main reasons they stay with their organisation are "the friendly people I work with…..great team spirit….and everybody helps each other when we've got a special project to finish for a customer". For many people, social interaction and working together are key "rewards" of work. The lack of day-to-day social interaction is often cited as one of the downsides of working from home.

But employees' perceptions of their organisation are also shaped significantly by their day-to-day contact with their line managers.[2] This is hardly surprising because it's managers who bring the organisation's HR and business policies to life. The way in which managers exercise their own discretion as to how they put these policies into practice has a direct effect on how employees feel about their job and the workplace more generally. Employees want to feel able to voice their views, to feel that managers listen to their ideas and value their contributions. Managers' behaviour can produce exactly that reaction or it can produce exactly the opposite result – dispirited, disinterested and de-motivated employees. Judged by the number of times I've seen the latter reflected in employee opinion surveys, the negative reaction occurs far too often. Good manager-employee relationships are central to performance management and fair performance reviews (Chapters 3 & 4 respectively). Great managers inspire people to be their best; poor managers inspire people to leave!

Managers in The Together Company, like managers elsewhere, are not perfect and they never will be. However, so strong is their belief that if you build your people first, the rest – customer satisfaction and financial success – will follow. And there are some very specific things that they aspire to.

What an effective manager must "be"

First, let's look at these in terms of what an effective manager must be. You can probably draw up your own list of things, like the one that follows, based on your experience of effective managers. My list[3] is shown below. It gives ten, very behaviourally focused characteristics which I believe are at the core of good manager-employee working relationships.

What an effective manager must be
A good communicator
A good listener
A magnet for talent
Comfortable with allowing other people to take the credit
Even-handed and even-tempered
Genuine
Sensitive to personal issues
Transparent, not opaque
Unquestionably honest

This list isn't rocket science – it's good, practical "common sense". It probably accounts for a significant proportion of the business success of a manager too. So, if a manager in your organisation wants to improve the performance of their team, he / she should start by asking others (peers or those managed directly) how well they (the manager) live up to these ten characteristics. This could be done either on a one-to-one basis or through small group meetings or, if people might be reluctant to express their views openly, via a short questionnaire which is completed anonymously. The results should provide a valuable insight about any contradictions between how the manager sees himself / herself and how others see the manager.

This analysis, in itself, should be a powerful self-development tool for the manager. If similar patterns of results appear across a representative cross section of managers, these should be brought to the attention of business leaders. When there are no contradictions about what a manager must be this should be praised. Particularly positive aspects, such as "a good communicator" and "a good listener", or proven ways to resolve perception differences between employees and managers, should be built into manager training programmes. Telling employees how the contradictions are being addressed is important otherwise they'll feel the whole exercise was a waste of time.

What a manager must "do"

Second, let's look at what managers must do. I've taken for granted that managers are responsible for meeting appropriate business objectives and basic standards in relation to monitoring budgets, conducting performance reviews and workload planning. My interest here is what they must do from the perspective of working relationships. Again, I've assembled a list of ten things.[4]

What a manager must do
Actively help people with their personal development
Allow people to learn from their mistakes without retribution
Allow people to speak out no matter what their role is
Always do what you say you are going to do
Give credit where credit is due
Put yourself in your employees' shoes and know what they are going through
Never become detached
Respect confidences
Show enthusiasm and drive; they are infectious and addictive
Treat people as adults

To what extent do employees in your organisation think managers do these things?

How do managers feel they measure up to the list? Where are the contradictions? A consultation exercise similar to that for "what an effective manager must be" would be worthwhile for the same reasons.

Many of the ten things are related. For example, the best managers In The Together Company are totally committed to developing their people, so they know what employees are going through and don't become detached. This was ably demonstrated to me recently by employees who took part in focus groups at one of my clients. They told me: "Managers here do a great job at bringing through and developing people at the lower levels in the organisation. This makes these people feel they are just as valued as other people in more senior jobs and earning lots more money."

My experience tells me that not doing the ten things is virtually guaranteed to alienate employees from their manager. When that happens, employees feel pigeon-holed with nowhere to go – hardly a rewarding workplace.

Role quality / job satisfaction

Lots of employees I meet tell me they really enjoy their job. When that happens, I believe they work smarter and stay longer than employees who don't. So, what is it about their job that makes them enjoy their work? A satisfying job has three characteristics[5]:

- It's intrinsically enjoyable, which is related to the nature of the work performed
- It provides an opportunity for personal growth and development
- It makes employees feel effective in terms of what they achieve.

Intrinsic job satisfaction

Intrinsic satisfaction is about five things. These are set out below:

Role clarity

First, make sure employees actually know what to do. This is part of performance management in The Together Company. It takes place when people join the company and it continues when either their current job changes significantly or they take on another role. Employees have clearly defined roles and responsibilities and they understand their importance. Remember that by involving employees in developing its vision and values, Accor Hotels, UK communicated what matters most to the company – and that provided the context for everybody's job.

Interest

Second, the job should be interesting. Of course, what one employee finds interesting, another may find boring. Interest arises when employees' jobs are stimulating and involving, because what's required is consistent with their interests. A customer-facing job like a checkout clerk at a supermarket for example, would suit a person who likes dealing face-to face with the public but doesn't want too much clerical responsibility. A software developer, on the other hand, will be looking for work that is challenging, relatively complex and involves novel situations where precise standards of excellence have to be met and they have to be a proactive problem solver. A senior manager will want a combination of technical or commercial challenges which stretches their abilities across all aspects of their work – perhaps involving building lasting relationships with key stakeholders and external contacts.

Autonomy

The third aspect of role quality / job satisfaction is autonomy. This is the degree of discretion given to employees to make decisions in line with their experience and the risks involved, rather than them always having to abide by the book – in other words, empowerment. Ideally, decision making authority should be cascaded to the lowest level possible in the organisation, so that employees resolve day-to-day problems when they arise and act in the best interests of customers, and do so with appropriate speed. Autonomy is also about employees having enough space to do what they do best. Managers in The Together Company give coaching which concentrates on building an employee's strengths rather than turning around their weaknesses[6] (some employees may not be for "turning"). This encourages employees to come up with new ideas and extend the boundaries of their capabilities.

Access to business leaders and customers

The fourth aspect is to allow exposure to business leaders in the organisation and to customers. Too often employees feel isolated from the people at the top of the organisation; sometimes they don't see or hear from them at all. That's because either the organisation is very large or business leaders are too busy and don't believe employee communication is their responsibility. In today's world of technology and work, where employees choose the organisation they want to work for, these reasons are ill-judged and unacceptable.

But it shouldn't be this way. All senior managers at one of my hotel clients employing around 1,000 people, hold bi-monthly meetings with employees to discuss business performance and employees concerns. A summary of the issues raised and agreed actions is sent to all Board members.

Two other examples come from the "Best Companies" lists.[7,8] At Assael Architects, a 68 employee firm of architects, Managing Director John Assael interviews all job applicants and mentors students. Browne Jacobson, a 500 employee legal firm, has introduced, at the request of employees, facilities where employees can meet informally with clients.

Appreciation

The fifth and final aspect is timely acknowledgement and appreciation for the work employees do. This is made possible by managers, so the manager-employee relationship is crucial. Notes of thanks from the manager, a personal letter from a senior manager, a visit from a director; all can be important at the right time. A General Manager of one of the hotels in the 1,000 employee client company mentioned above, shows lots of appreciation of the work employees do for guests, by making impromptu visits to the department, presenting small gifts, and spending time with them to talk about their achievements. The General Manager's personal commitment to appreciation emerged strongly in employee focus groups which I ran as part of a total reward strategy review. Many more ideas for showing appreciation and steps to creating successful recognition are set out in Chapter 13, Recognition and celebration.

Personal growth and development

One of the best things The Together Company does for employees is to help them get better. This can involve on-the-job activities, such as working on a special project or having access to a group of talented, knowledgeable employees who share their experiences. Inviting gurus to give in-company presentations about leading-edge topics or arranging a visit to a university or business school are two examples which often work well.

Personal growth in Together Companies is an important part of performance management. We saw earlier in the book how companies like David Lloyd Leisure incorporate personal development plans into their performance review process. Appropriate skills based training to keep employees up-to-date about for example, new processes for ordering supplies, operating new office equipment, health and safety changes or IT systems, is important too.

Personal effectiveness

People need to feel that they are doing a good job. We are unlikely to really engage with our work if we believe this will result in failure. On the other hand, if we believe we can successfully achieve a task, we will make the effort required and persist, even though we face obstacles along the way. One of the best ways of building such self-belief is through successive, progressively difficult assignments in different situations. This allows employees to succeed as an individual and to see that they are getting progressively better. Constructive feedback (Chapter 4, Fair performance review) play a crucial role here.

Physical environment

Imagine you're a complete stranger to your working environment. What would it tell you about your organisation – about what it does and how it does it? It could convey, for example, "A frantic, paper-pushing factory where people sit at rows and rows of desks and appear to work independently". Or it might say: "This is a relaxed and creative place, where the work space layout and nearby social and informal meeting areas suggest people work together". Whatever the description is, it paints a picture of your organisation – a picture you may like or dislike. Some features of life at Microsoft are shown in Figure 14.1.

The Together Company recognises that today's workplace is one of the most significant tools in helping people be effective. Get it right and it can work wonders; get it wrong and it can stifle the business activities that matter most. The physical workplace affects us all – positively or negatively. While this book is not the right place for a discussion about feng shui, the principles of it (based on ancient Chinese philosophy) provide us with some interesting and, dare I say common sense, guidance about the physical work space:

- Use curves instead of straight lines
- Brightness outweighs darkness – make the most of natural light
- People shouldn't sit with their backs to the door or face blank walls
- Colour may be used to support themes – light blue for calm, red to encourage energy
- Mirrors should be used to reflect light and good views.

FIGURE 14.1   Microsoft: A Comfortable Working Environment[9]

More than just providing comfortable work stations, notebook mobility and state-of-the-art meeting rooms with the latest AV facilities, we take care of the broader work environment.

Our aim is simply to make everyone feel as stress-free as possible whilst they are at work, so they can focus on doing their best. Here are some of the facilities you'll find at our Thames Valley Park campus:

- Four coffee shops to sit and drink in – which come in very handy for some of the informal meetings that our open culture encourages
- An airy restaurant serving a wide selection of great food
- Landscaped gardens, with lake, putting green and croquet – there are also picnic facilities available in the summer, just the place to enjoy your free ice creams
- Shop offering dry cleaning, photo processing and video / DVD rental
- Cash machines, on-site banking and independent financial advisors
- Waitrose delivery service – shop on-line and pick up your groceries before you leave for home
- Wireless environment to allow you to be online anywhere in the building, including by the lake
- Chill-out zones to unwind and relax in
- Independently-operated day nursery facility
- Independent "Wellbeing" centre offering a range of healthcare services and advice, including alternative therapies and massage.

Latest Technology – as Standard

We put the latest technology into the hands of our own people. It's important for us to be a living case study when it comes to using our software – so our employees can talk about it from first-hand experience.

We provide our employees with the following:

- The fastest broadband connection and wireless at work, and at home should they require it
- The latest mobile devices and smart phones
- All our latest software.

Rewarding work layouts[10]

The Together Company believes that if the work space is to be rewarding, that is, pleasant, energising, supportive and effective, it must reflect the way people work. There are essentially three ways that they do:

- Extensively desk-based – such as administrative or customer-facing groups
- Primarily office-based but often in meetings or away from their desk – for example, technical or managerial employees
- Frequently away from their office, but need work space when they return – such as sales employees or senior executives.

Many of the new work layouts, such as groups of desks, study booths, informal meeting areas, formal meeting rooms, breakout space for project or teamworking activities and quiet areas are shared. This requires news ways of working, such as adjusting works layouts to suit individual needs, a clean-desk policy when people leave and booking use of work space. Without this, people will not be able to perform their work effectively, so it may become non-rewarding. Sometimes it's the little things which matter most to people – the tea machines and the comfort of chairs in informal meeting and quiet areas, so getting these right matters too. The moral of the story is "involve employees from the start".

The benefits of a rewarding work environment

Just because you've set up a great office layout which everybody is raving about doesn't mean it will automatically stay that way. You need to monitor how it's working for the business and for employees – togetherness. Hard measures such as savings on property, heating, water and lighting, and ability to accommodate new employees as a result of business growth are, in my view, "givens". In terms of a rewarding work environment, soft measures are the most significant. The working environment at Feather Brooksbank, an 85 employee media agency based in Edinburgh, is open-plan with everyone, including managing directors and the board, sitting together. This encourages employees to feel they can contribute to all areas of the business[11].

Other examples of soft measures, which could be measured relatively easily through an employee satisfaction or engagement survey, focus groups or pulse surveys, are:

- Visibility of business leaders
- Employer image
- Employee motivation and productivity

● Transfer of knowledge.

Is it right for you?

A rewarding workplace is right for all Together Companies, whatever the organisational circumstances. Good manager-employee relationships should be the aim always – the ten characteristics of what a manager must "be" and what a manager must "do" (set out earlier in this chapter) should not be compromised. Clear responsibilities, interesting work (ask employees how they feel – don't assume they find the work they do interesting) and giving people the power to make decisions, within appropriate guidelines and risk, all make for a rewarding workplace. My top ten other suggestions for creating one are set out below:

1. Highly visible business leaders who "walk the talk". In small companies the MD could hold "breakfast clubs" at the main location to discuss business issues and employee concerns. In large businesses the heads of business units could do the same. Additionally, all new employees, as part of their induction, spend an hour with the MD or head of business unit. In small companies each employee might have a mentor on the Board.
2. Leading edge technology for technology people – enable them to test your products / services; this can be invaluable later when they're contacting customers.
3. Access to gurus or others, inside and outside your organisation, with appropriate knowledge from whom they can learn.
4. Opportunity to work on a challenging / key project.
5. Encourage employees to share their ideas and concerns.
6. Allow employees the autonomy that can lead to rapid career growth and recognition.
7. Opportunity to give something back to the local community or environment.
8. Make employees feel appreciated – never take them for granted. If you do, they'll go elsewhere.
9. Make sure your physical work environment says what you want it to say. Plants and colours never hurt anyone! If you want creativity – give people the space and relaxing areas to be creative.
10. Ask employees what matters to them – sometimes it's the little things that really count!

Key points

- A rewarding workplace is about far more than pay and benefits: it's about the manager-employee relationship, role quality / job satisfaction and the physical work environment.
- What an effective manager must "be" probably accounts for a significant proportion of the business success of a manager, so if you want to improve performance, start with the ten characteristics "what a manager must be". Then look at "what a manager must do".
- Employees who enjoy their job work smarter and stay longer than employees who don't. So, make sure:
  - You provide work which is "intrinsically satisfying" – that's related to the nature of the work employees do
  - You give employees opportunities for personal growth and development
  - Employees feel effective in terms of what they achieve – that often comes down to recognition and praise and "doing a job that's worthwhile"
- The physical work environment says a lot about your organisation – about what it does and how it does it. Make sure it says the right things for you – teamwork, creativity and a great place to be.

CHAPTER FIFTEEN
Reward communications

Communicating Total Reward at The Royal Bank of Scotland Group

The Royal Bank of Scotland Group (RBS) communicates extensively with employees. Communications are designed to inform employees about what's important to the business, what they can expect to receive in return for working at RBS and the Group's employment policies and procedures.

RBS communicates in lots of different ways, from brochures to the Group intranet, and from an HR contact centre to personal statements about total reward. Examples of what it does are set out below.

Targeting prospective employees

RBS doesn't just communicate with current employees. The Group's website www.rbs.com includes a section about what the Group offers employees – salaries and benefits, learning and development and work-life balance. Each of these contains outlines of the programmes offered. The Group's Total Reward approach is described, along with case studies of how some employees have tailored their reward package, through RBSelect, the Group's benefits choice plan, to suit their needs.

Explaining the employment offer

When RBS makes an employment offer, the successful applicant receives a copy of "Starting Out", a guide to working at RBS. Starting Out has sections about:

- RBS – its business and brands
- Total Reward – the Group's approach to pay and benefits
- Linking pay to performance – key principles and the role of bonus and incentives
- Tailoring their own package – increasing the value through RBSelect
- Pension and other benefits, such as employee share schemes and preferential rate banking products
- Starting work – information on what happens during induction
- Employment policies – introduction to employment procedures and policies, such as sickness absence, grievance and discipline.

RBS asks successful applicants to take time to consider their offer carefully, because it wants to make sure people understand what's being offered and what's expected in return.

Helping people settle in

To help people settle in and find their way around, employees begin an induction programme. They meet colleagues and are introduced to the RBS intranet and other sources of information on employment and business policies and procedures.

At an appropriate point the employee's manager discusses the Group's Performance Management programme for the division where the employee works and agrees with them a set of performance objectives and Personal Development Plan for the coming year. This helps build up a picture of the skills and competencies the employee needs to perform the job effectively and to identify the support they will need to meet their agreed objectives.

Managers also explain incentive and bonus programmes that the employee is eligible for, both within the division and the Group as a whole.

Giving employees access to Group policies and procedures

All employees have access to the RBS Group intranet, which provides comprehensive details of employment policies and procedures. These include:

- RBSelect – the benefits choice programme and all offers through RBSelect Offers and One-Off Election.
- YourBank – banking services at exclusive preferential rates for employees
- YourTime – different ways of working and flexible working arrangements
- YourCar – the car purchase or lease scheme for all employees
- Give As You Earn – the payroll-giving scheme

employees, irrespective of whether or not they are eligible for the reward programme. Very few reward practices fall into the "totally confidential" category these days. These sessions can help build a climate of trust and inspire employees to become eligible for such rewards in the future. Frequently asked question and answer sheets, tailored to various locations if appropriate, should be included.

E-communications

Many organisations have invested heavily in e-communications. A few intend to move to an electronic-only based system for communicating HR information to employees. Some of the most interesting, and potentially the most powerful e-communications, are on-line modelling tools. These enable managers in The Together Company to model performance-based salary reviews and see how employees' bonus payments, for example, will be affected by company and individual performance.

Some organisations have separate intranets for business leaders, which show on an individual and totally confidential basis, the current value of all shares and / or share options held by the business leader, bonus received and deferred bonus payments. Additionally, each business leader can see how a change in their base salary and performance (the organisation's performance and theirs) will affect share awards in the future. Employee-based sites are popular too. Flexible benefits choices, total reward statements, HR policies and information about work-life programmes feature regularly.

E-communications offer organisations cost savings through reduction in postage, printing, hardware and software maintenance and more efficient use of service centres. That's fine if all employees currently have or eventually will have access to an intranet site. But the customer experience in many organisations suggests people want more than the "call-centre, telephone-queuing, look-up-our website" approach.

Print communications

The Together Company, unlike the many companies who believe technology is the only way to communicate today, doesn't underestimate the positive impact of print communications. Many people like to have something they can look at when they want to – on a train, at home, with their families or work colleagues and they may not use a computer at work or have one at home. If someone's been working on a lap-top all day, they may be glad to get away from it at home!

When print communications, for example posters, are placed in prominent places at work, they serve as powerful and regular reminders of specific reward programmes, such as work-life options and share schemes or, very importantly, your organisation's values. They are there for customers and visitors to see too – conveying what matters most to your organisation.

Multi-faceted communications

While the popularity of E-communications has increased significantly during the last five years The Together Company adopts a multi-faceted approach – balancing high-tech and high touch – which is tailored to the target employee audience. Three examples illustrate this point:

- Explanations about the annual pay increase are often best given face-to-face and supported in writing
- Giving employees several ways to enroll for a flexible benefits programme (over the company's intranet, by telephoning a contact centre or filling in a form) is more flexible for them and more administratively efficient for you, than relying on a single method
- Launching a flexible benefits programme by producing hard copy and electronic versions of the scheme brochure, circulating briefing documents electronically to managers and holding a series of road shows, will enable you to reach employees throughout the organisation quickly and personally.

Step 3: Measuring the impact

How often does your organisation measure the impact of reward communications? If you don't, you may be wasting money. If you do, what measures do you use? Typical measures used by The Together Company are set out below:

Understanding of programme: Employees could be asked to indicate the extent to which they agree or disagree with several statements such as:

- I understand how my job has been graded
- I understand how my base salary increase is calculated
- I know how pay rates compare to market rates
- I know the competencies for my job
- I know the financial value of my total reward package – base pay, bonus and benefits choice.

Changes in behaviour: Switching to on-line enrolment for flexible benefits or asking managers for more information about performance based pay.

Employees' perceptions: The reward communication's impact, including awareness of internally-branded programmes, for example Sharesave.

Increased trust: Trust in the organisation's leadership. Employees could be asked to indicate the extent to which they agree or disagree with statements such as:

- I feel that flexible benefits offer me a real financial benefit
- I feel that our team bonus is designed to save money for the organisation rather than improve everybody's performance
- My manager holds me back from promotions
- The decisions my manager takes my about my rewards are fair.

Value of communications: A cost/benefit analysis, assessed by a comparison of the cost of the reward communication and the results from the other measures mentioned above.

Ways of measuring the impact of reward communications vary from the very simple, such as employee focus groups, interviews and informal discussions, to paper or electronic surveys. The decision about which to use depends on factors such as ease of reaching the target audience, the need for background information about why employees feel they way they do, the purpose of the survey (to make decisions or "test employee opinion), cost and timescale.

Dealing with negative reactions to communications

What happens if your reward communication doesn't go according to plan and some people react negatively? After all, few, if any, communications are "perfect". In most organisations there are some people who I call "high-maintenance" – they are cynics, who criticise the motives of the organisation, whatever it does. So, when your organisation decides for example, to introduce a performance based pay plan and communicate the details to employees (after their involvement in the design by the way) the cynics see it as a company ploy to deliver less pay or increase the amount of non-pensionable pay, so it can save money at the expense of employees. This is in stark contrast to your objective of tying together the success of people (individual and team contributions) and the fortunes of the company.

Similarly, a negative reaction occurs when you start consulting about changes to pensions for example: "This is a sham – the company has made its mind up about what it's going to do, so why bother to consult us!" These negative reactions have potential for disruption if the cynics start to spread their propaganda and deliberately distort or "rubbish" your organisation's good intentions.

Ideally, of course, these employees don't exist in The Together Company, but let's assume that your company is aspiring to become one and you've got a few cynics around, and in the past they've been disruptive. How should you deal with them? Negative reactions can arise as a result of either inappropriate communications or human characteristics, that is, some people are more keen or inclined than others to respond negatively. So, if you're planning a reward communication make sure you follow the three step process to successful reward communications set out above. This way reward communications will be appropriate and potential questions will have been answered. However, if you've communicated already and experienced some negative reactions, first have a critical look at what you did and how you did it. In relation to the three step process set out above, ask yourself five key questions:

1. Was the purpose of the communication set out clearly?
2. Was the language "employee-friendly" – plain English not jargon?
3. From an employee standpoint, did you answer the question "What's in this for me?"
4. How did employees feel about the method of communications – about right, remote and impersonal?
5. If you want to repeat the communication, would you use the same method? If not, what would you do differently and why?

If you're satisfied that you did the best possible job, the cynics with their instinctively negative attitude are likely to be source of "discontent", so check where the negative reactions come from to make sure you're right. What should you do about them? If they're really disruptive and there's evidence of gross misconduct, then follow your disciplinary procedure and take legal advice! Hopefully, it won't come to that, but remember that while exemplar employees are good role models, cynics are bad ones and need to be discouraged vehemently!

Case study

Reward communication at Accor Hotels

With 168,000 employees (called associates) in 140 countries, Accor is the European leader and one of the world's largest groups in Hotels and Services. Its brands include Novotel, Sofitel and Mercure, and budget-priced hotel chains such as Ibis and Formule 1 with 92 Hotels in the UK & Ireland. Accor UK employs around 3,000 people.

Under the banner "Succeeding Together through Teamwork", Accor UK communicates its vision, values and key elements of the rewards and benefits employees will receive, in a simple, two-sided leaflet, which is given to all employees. The rewards and benefits that Accor is committed to providing employees with, while they are employed with Accor UK, are set out under five broad headings.

Your Wages

- The salary for your position will be competitive in comparison to similar jobs in the local area.
- Accor has established a salary which is above the National Minimum Wage which is applicable to all permanent team members following the successful completion of their probationary period.
- If you are requested to work extra hours (outside contracted hours) this will be compensated for either by time off or by payment.
- Your salary will be reviewed at least once a year, in the light of your performance and responsibilities and prevailing market conditions.
- If you work on a bank holiday you will be paid double time plus a day off in lieu.

Your Hours of Work and Rest

- Accor wants you to strike a reasonable balance between work and home life – you will not be expected to work excessive hours.
- You are entitled to a minimum of 20 days holiday for each full calendar year worked (January to December), up to a maximum of 25 days plus Bank Holidays.
- Special Leave – depending on your length of service you are entitled to extra paid leave in special circumstances: marriage, birth of your child, moving house and bereavement.
- You will receive two full days off per week (average over four-week period).
- Your shift patterns are dictated by levels of business. However, we guarantee that you will be treated fairly.

You and your Manager

- We operate an Open Door policy. Your Manager will listen to you and welcomes your comments and suggestions.
- Your Manager will communicate with you and pass all the on information you need to do your job.
- Your Manager will provide you with all the necessary tools to do your job.

- Your Manager will give you regular feedback on how you are doing and coach you where necessary.
- Your Manager will keep you informed on the performance of your department, hotel and Accor.
- You will be invited to attend periodic "open table" meetings with members of the management team and will be able to ask questions of concern to you.

Your Training and Development

- You will be given the opportunity to undertake at least one training programme each year.
- You will be given opportunities to fulfil your personal development plan and have access to a PC to investigate career moves via the Accor jobs recruitment site.
- Accor is committed to providing training to Company Standards for all individuals across the brands (e.g. Progrès / Players).
- Appraisals take place at least once a year and you will have an interview with your Manager to discuss your performance, training needs and development plans.
- Other training opportunities – if there is a particular course or qualification which you wish to work towards, which the hotel sees as appropriate, you may be given assistance with the fees.
- You will have access to a dedicated PC situated in the hotel which you can use to follow various e-learning training programmes.

Your Benefits

- Uniforms provided by Accor will be dry cleaned by the company, except for shirts and blouses.
- A social event for staff will normally be organised and held during the course of the year.
- Eye test vouchers – where VDU work forms the major part of your daily work routine then you are entitled to a periodic free eye test.
- Where meals on duty are provide they will be of a good quality.
- Accor operates a discretionary company sick pay scheme for all those with 6 months or more service.
- "Be our best headhunter" – if you introduce someone who is hired by us you will receive £150 gross after the person has successfully completed 3 months service.
- Accor Card – after one year's service you are entitled to significant discounts at other Accor properties worldwide.

- Accor provides the opportunity for you to work in different brands and to transfer to different countries.
- Family Life Solutions – provides a free and confidential helpline for advice on family matters available to all members of staff and their families.
- Pensions – after one year's service you will be entitled to join the Accor Retirement Benefit Plan.
- Periodically you will have the opportunity to participate in "Accor en Actions", our employee share ownership

Is it right for you?

While reward communications should always be simple, irrespective of the size or type of organisation, large organisations, by sheer numbers of employees and range of reward practices, are more likely than small organisations, to communicate more information about reward and do so more often. Here are some suggestions about approach.

Small organisation

A simple, hard copy leaflet, say four sides of A4, could contain the key points about everything to do with reward. The sections might be:

- How your salary is calculated
- The performance review process
- The benefits package
    - Pension scheme – eligibility and contributions
    - Life assurance
    - Sick pay
    - Holidays
- Recognition – informal awards and what they're given for
- Working pattern choices – an overview
- Profit sharing bonus – what it's paid for and how it's calculated
- Company social events.

The leaflet could include a calendar showing what your organisation has done during the last year and what it plans to do this year. Typical items could be "review salaries in April, "calculate the company profit share" in June and hold the "Christmas Party / themed night" in December".

Fairly large organisation

You could also produce a leaflet along the lines of that for the small organisation, although the contents probably need to be more comprehensive (see Accor case study at the end of this chapter). But the size and structure of your organisation probably lends itself to a multi-channel approach along the following lines:

- Key reward policies posted on your HR intranet site
- Booklets and / or fact sheets on key reward practices – these could be made available in hard copy and electronic forms
- Reward is a "standing item" on regular team briefing
- Questions about employees' understanding of reward practices included in an annual employee opinion survey.

Key points

- Craft a compelling message – communicate what matters most about reward, to the organisation and to employees.
- Balance high and high touch – don't underestimate the positive impact of so-called traditional approaches, such as hard copy brochures and posters.
- Measure the impact of reward communications – you need to know what works best.
- Remember – your organisation's website says a lot about its "style". What the site says about reward tells people what you value most. That's a powerful recruitment tool.

CHAPTER SIXTEEN

The five business reasons to become a Together Company

At the beginning of this book I said:

"The world of work has changed forever. The balance of power has shifted irreversibly from the organisation to the employee. To compete in this world, business leaders need to know how to engage and motivate talented people and ensure their commitment to business goals. To compete in this world, you have to become a Together Company."

But what are the business benefits of doing all the things I've covered in the book – of becoming a Together Company? Where's the proof that any of it makes employees more engaged and that engagement turns into improved business results? I believe we have to look no further than the results of a few highly-successful organisations – all of whom make substantial investments in their employees. Note the word "investments": too many businesses still consider employees to be a "cost", a cost which should be reduced whenever an opportunity arises. This is a far cry from the philosophy of The Together Company where the focus is maximising the return-on-investment (ROI) in employees – an investment which is often the largest it makes. And that ROI manifests itself in the five business reasons to become a Together Company.

The five business reasons to become a Together Company
1. Working smarter / working together
2. Satisfied customers
3. Profits and growth
4. Thinking like owners
5. Great place to work

Working smarter / working together

At the heart of The Together Company are employees who are committed to the organisation, employees who work smarter and work together to create truly outstanding organisational performance. This is what Cadbury Schweppes is all about. In 2004 when the company was named Britain's "Most Admired Company", Todd Stitzer, Chief Executive Officer commented[1]:

"Our success is driven by our unrelenting focus on working together to create brands people love and a strong commitment to values that run through all aspects of our business."

In 2005 the company swept the board at Human Resources magazine's HR Excellence awards, winning:

- Best HR contribution to merger and acquisition
- Best HR contribution to business strategy, and
- The Overall HR Excellence award.

Bob Stack, Chief HR Officer, Cadbury Schweppes, commented[2]:

"Over the past three years we have been through some radical changes. These began with the appointment of a new CEO, Todd Stitzer, and the announcement of the acquisition of Adams and culminated in the introduction of sweeping structural and cultural changes that would pave the way for future growth.

We know that such transformational change can put added pressures on employees. However, we have been able to use this backdrop of change to fuel our highest ever levels of employee commitment that's influenced our success and performance."

During this time the share price rose by 80% and Cadbury Schweppes' first global employee satisfaction survey found that 95% were proud to work for the company. 2005 was an excellent year for business results too – revenue growth at 6% is the best Cadbury Schweppes has seen in over a decade and profits before tax were up 12%.

Bob Stack added:

"I'm extremely proud of the HR team – it's a great credit to them that their teamwork and integration stood out from in a competitive and impressive line up of leaders in this field."

Cadbury Schweppes[3] places great importance on rewarding the continuously improving performance of its employees. Its approach supports the company's team environment and collaborative work style. Rewards are not only financial, but they come through training and career opportunities, and flexible packages that reflect employees' life changes. The company's incentive plans pay out on the basis of business and personal performance and annual pay reviews take personal performance into account too. Rewards, again, which reflect the needs of people and the organisation– togetherness.

Satisfied customers

Reward practices based on the delivery of results to customers feature in many organisations. At MBNA's customer service call centre, for example, hundreds of employees provide personalised service to the holders of credit cards issued by the company. A high level of service is a key driver of cardholder usage and loyalty, so MBNA measures customer satisfaction daily. Scores are posted daily and rewards are accumulated daily but paid monthly. The aim is to give each team a fresh start every day towards winning a reward[4].

Tesco's[5] core purpose is "to create value for customers to earn their lifetime loyalty". Its success depends on people – those who shop with Tesco and those who work with Tesco. The company measures its performance through a management tool called the Steering Wheel, which is divided into four quadrants – Customer, Operations, People and Finance. Each quadrant is divided into parts which have a set of key performance indicators (KPIs). The remuneration of senior management is linked to the KPIs, with bonuses paid on a sliding scale of achievement on the Steering Wheel[6].

But it's not only senior management who benefit financially from Tesco's success. Sir Terry Leahy, Chief Executive, commenting on employees sharing a £111m save-as-you-earn payout said[7]:

"I am delighted that so many staff chose to do this and so share in the success that they help achieve through all their hard work."

The commercial success of Tesco speaks for itself.

Profits and growth

Without financial success and growth, there can't be a Together Company – certainly not in the long term. Strong income growth is a recurring theme of its results and is a key source of investment in its future – a future based on delivering results that matter most to shareholders, customers and employees. The Royal Bank of Scotland

Group (RBS) has a good track record on all three counts[8,9]:

- RBS 2005 business highlights included profit before tax up 21%, total income up 14%, customer growth in all divisions and total dividend up 25%
- RBS was voted Best for Overall Customer Service category, 2005 Personal Finance and Savings Readership Awards
- RBS Retail Banking has been voted one of the top 20 Best Big Companies to Work For 2006.

Ultimately, these successes come down to people. In 2006, Sir Fred Goodwin, Group Chief Executive, said[10]:

"In the 2005 Employee Opinion Survey the Group improved its score in each of the 14 categories surveyed. At 86%, response to the 2005 Employee Opinion Survey was even higher than previously. We have launched new initiatives to encourage innovation and leadership. Our new Business School and programmes developed in conjunction with Harvard Business School are helping to develop the vision and quality of management that the Group will need in challenging markets in the future."

RBS is recognised as having one of the most innovative and flexible reward schemes in the financial services sector. Reward and recognition are part of the Group's employee proposition which is designed to attract, engage and retain the best talent[11]. The Group has developed a human capital model that correlates a range of HR metrics with business metrics. The Group believes that a successful reward programme is one that recognises the specific needs of its various business units – and of the people who work in them. This is the very essence of The Together Company.

Thinking like owners

Creating a culture in which people feel energised, valued and rewarded – fairly and competitively – for their contribution to business success, is a "given" for The Together Company. When this happens, I believe people start to feel – sometimes sub-consciously, sometimes overtly – that they have a personal stake in the business and, given time, actually start to "think like owners". This is a highly-prized goal of Together Companies and I believe there's no better example of this than The John Lewis Partnership – the UK's largest example of worker co-ownership. All 64,000 permanent employees are Partners in the business.

Culture is a driver of reward policy at The John Lewis Partnership. The highest paid person in the Partnership can't earn more than 25 times the salary of the lowest person. Not only that there are no long-term incentive plans because these would be inconsistent with the culture[12].

Employee benefits[13] include John Lewis and Waitrose store discounts, a non-contributory final salary pension scheme, payable from 60, to most Partners who have completed a five-year qualifying period and subsidised holiday accommodation for Partners with at least three years' service. The reward package also includes an annual bonus which is a proportion of the business's profits - in 2006 this was the equivalent of eight weeks' pay. Has such profit sharing been at the expense of customers? Far from it! In January 2006, John Lewis and Waitrose took first and second place in a new survey "Consumer Satisfaction Index 2006[14]. In addition, the company believes that the commitment of Partners to the business is a unique source of competitive advantage which has fuelled 75 years of profitable growth and a reputation amongst customers and suppliers unparalleled in the UK retail industry[15].

Great place to work

There's an increasing body of evidence that shows great workplaces help attract and retain the best people and are good for business. "Best Companies" surveys[16] provide lots of examples which include:

- W L Gore & Associates, manufacturer of Gore-Tex breathable, waterproof fabric used in clothing worn by skiers and walkers, and used in medical products developed by the company's scientists and engineers, has taken the No 1 spot in the Sunday Times list for the third year successive year. The firm, which made profits of £14.6m last financial year on its UK revenue of £105.9m, and employs 425 people, achieved a 83% positive score (the second highest in the survey) for happiness with pay and benefits. Associates (employees) help decide their colleagues' pay. Now that says a lot about trust!
- Bacardi-Martini, the Southampton-based drinks manufacturer, employing 450 people, has one of the strongest records in the Sunday Times list, finishing in the top 10 in each of the last five years. Happiness with pay and benefits earns the company a 74% positive score and a top 10 ranking on these practices.
- DLA Piper, named Law Firm of the Year in 2005, has been highly ranked in the Financial Times "50 Best Workplaces in the UK" as well as being named one of the "100 Best Workplaces in Europe". Andrew Darwin, UK Managing Partner, said[17]:

"I am truly delighted by this news. We provide legal advice to some of the world's best and to do this we have to demand a lot of our people, but in return we have tried to create a great working environment. I think the results speak for themselves."

AstraZeneca[18], one of the UK's leading healthcare companies, understands that success depends on providing its people with a working environment in which they can create, solve, challenge and improve. The company aims to be an innovative leader in everything it does and its reward programme is no exception. AstraZeneca has a performance culture, where individuals and teams are rewarded for their ideas and contribution to the company's success – ideas which can make a difference in all aspects of the business. The reward programme includes flexible benefits and a shares and cash bonus plan which blends company performance, with function / business unit and individual / team success. In February 2006, AstraZeneca released its full year results[19] for 2005 – profit before tax up 38%, and "strong growth from key products and improved efficiency drive a 44% increase in earnings per share for 2005".

Case study

Rewarding change at Scottish Water

Some of you may be surprised that my last case study comes from the public sector. But many private sector companies would be proud to achieve what Scottish Water has achieved in such a short time. Scottish Water was formed in April 2002 following the merger of the three former water utilities – East, West and North of Scotland. Each utility had its own way of doing things – different people practices, different terms of employment and different reward practices. Today, things are very different and the business achievements speak for themselves. So, let me tell their story.

Scottish Water, a publicly-owned business answerable to the Scottish Parliament, faces some tough challenges. Between 2002 and 2006, its key challenges were:

- To begin the rebuild and replacement of worn-out infrastructure
- To improve customer service levels and ensure standards are consistent across Scotland
- To accelerate the pace of capital investment in order to meet new stringent European Union directives which will improve drinking water quality and better protect the environment.

Tough efficiency targets have to be met too: reduce operating costs by 40% by 2006; and deliver the capital investment programme for £500m less than the original cost estimate. The people impact of these targets has been significant: fewer jobs (5,500 in 2002 to around 3,700 by 2006) and major revisions to terms and conditions such as working time, overtime, shift working, salary bands, pay progression, holidays and retirement.

Engaging people in the change process

From the outset, Scottish Water has worked in partnership with the trades unions and employees. It set up the Scottish Water Council, a company-wide body, and Business Unit Councils for each part of Scottish Water's business, to consider how the challenges and efficiency targets were going to be met. *"Initially, people were very suspicious"* says Andrew Walker, Head of Human Resources. *"Given the amount of change they were facing, that was hardly surprising, so we have put a lot of effort into engaging people in the change process."*

Scottish Water also set up working groups to look at everything they do and how they do it. The "how" aspect was particularly important. *"We realised early in the change process that if the business was to succeed, what really mattered was how people behaved"*, continues Andrew Walker, *"so one working group was tasked with developing a set of company values that would guide everybody at Scottish Water in how they go about their daily work"*. The four values – Involve People, Challenge for Benefit, Clear Conversation, and Deliver Promises – have a strong behavioural flavour (Figure 16.1) and their importance is shared throughout Scottish Water, from the Chief Executive to front line operative employees, from union representatives to managers, and from administrators to technical people.

Employee involvement hasn't stopped at working groups. Scottish Water has taken all employees away from the workplace twice. The first event was about visualising the change and how the company could get there. The second event was an internal trade fair with "stands" manned by employees. Each stand represented a different part of the business and employees explained to "visiting colleagues" what their department does. The whole event was designed to help everybody make connections between different parts of the business.

Rewarding individual performance and behaviour

Scottish Water's reward policy plays a key role in communicating to everybody what matters most to the business and how important "living the values" is to its success. It does this in two ways: first, through the performance management system; and second, through pay.

FIGURE 16.1   Scottish Water Values

Involve People	• Actively encouraging people to get involved in what's going on, especially in change
	• Ensuring everyone has an understanding of the bigger picture and is well motivated through that involvement
	• Helping people:
	    • Determine and shape their own future
	    • Value themselves and others
	    • Appreciate the value of customers
	    • Appreciate the value of teams

Challenge for Benefit	• Individuals and teams will challenge the norm, offering better alternatives, which deliver measurable benefits • Striving to develop best practice • Demonstrating the courage of our convictions
Clear Conversation	• Always checking for understanding and never assuming that a message is clear to all • Tailoring both message and style to suit an audience • Ensuring the communication method used suits the relevant target audience • Ensuring you know the facts before communicating and sticking to them • Being truthful
Deliver Promises	• Building confidence in customers' minds and showing we care about what we do • Making and meeting our promises, both internally and externally • Accepting and delivering our promises on public health • Accepting and delivering our promises on doing things at less cost • Not committing to actions unless we intend to carry them out

---

The performance management system, called "Star", which stands for "setting targets, achieving results", was developed by one of the working groups. Star covers everybody at Scottish Water and is about three things: company values, career development and rewards. Unlike many such systems, it's definitely not a one-off event. All employees have a Development Plan which sets out individual performance-related objectives and personal development or training to help them achieve their objectives and they discuss this with their manager on a quarterly basis.

The second aspect of communicating what matters most to Scottish Water is pay. The current 8% pay deal, which runs from 2004 to 2006, includes 1.5% for linking pay and performance through Star. This has a direct impact on the annual salary review for each employee. The employee's immediate line manager uses Star to assess two things:

- What has been achieved (outcomes) – actual performance against objectives
- How it has been achieved (behaviours) – the extent to which the employee has demonstrated their commitment to Scottish Water Values.

Each value has been developed to include statements of positive and negative behaviour – Figure 16.2 gives an example (shown first in Chapter 3, Performance management) – against which people are assessed.

FIGURE 16.2 Scottish Water Value "Involve People": Examples of behaviour	
Positive behaviour	*Negative behaviour*
• Uses feedback from others / team • Treats people with dignity, respect and fairness • Listens to others and fairly considers all ideas and opinions • Helps others in the team on own initiative • Involves the team to produce optimum solutions • Shares information openly • Raises issues and works with others to resolve them • Is open minded about different approaches to working • Recognises and takes account of the different strengths of team members	• Responds negatively to others • Fails to listen to and involve others • Allows personal considerations to cloud judgments • Doesn't consult people when appropriate • Actively works in isolation • Refuses to assist other team members in times of fluctuating workloads • Keeps ideas to themselves and takes credit where it's not due • Sticks to own ideas

An employee's commitment to the values is assessed on the four-point, frequency-based rating scale shown below:

1 = All	All positive indicators displayed every time without failure
2 = Most	Mostly positive indicators displayed but inconsistently, with 1 or 2 negative indicators
3 = Some	Some positive indicators occasionally, with 3 or 4 negative indicators
4 = Few	Almost all behaviours are negative, with 1 or 2 occasional positive indicators

The result of the manager's assessment is a simple overall STAR rating that covers outcomes and behaviours. There are four ratings which are referred to simply as 1 (the highest), 2, 3 (the minimum "expected" of everybody) and 4 (unsatisfactory).

Force fitting the number of employees in each rating to produce a preferred performance distribution isn't Scottish Water's style, although the company does monitor the percentage of employees in each of the Star rating categories.

The employee's Star rating is translated into a salary increase using a matrix that takes into account where they are currently paid in the salary band. This is done to ensure that a high performing employee with a salary in the low part of the range receives an increase greater than that given to a low performer whose salary is in the high part of the range. Figure 16.3 shows an example matrix. "X" is the increase given to an employee with a Star rating of 3 and a salary in the medium part of the range.

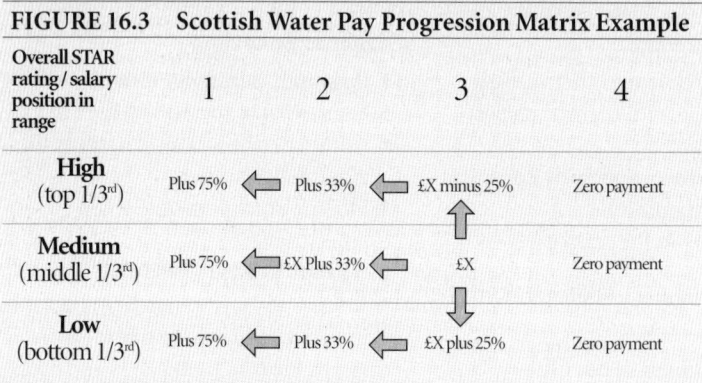

FIGURE 16.3   Scottish Water Pay Progression Matrix Example

Overall STAR rating / salary position in range	1	2	3	4
High (top 1/3rd)	Plus 75%	Plus 33%	£X minus 25%	Zero payment
Medium (middle 1/3rd)	Plus 75%	£X Plus 33%	£X	Zero payment
Low (bottom 1/3rd)	Plus 75%	Plus 33%	£X plus 25%	Zero payment

The company has also set up a working party to look at how employees use their skills and competencies and to consider whether these should be linked to reward.

Sharing in organisational success

All employees at Scottish Water are eligible for a performance related bonus too. There are two schemes, one for management and one for all other employees. Both schemes are linked to Scottish Water's six key performance areas – Customer Service, Customer Accounts, Quality and Environment, Assets, Financial and People. Targets in each of these areas are cascaded first to business unit level and then to each team within the business unit.

The management scheme pays out between 10% and 25% of salary, depending on personal performance, company results and the manager's role. The maximum payment under the all-employee scheme is £850 which is linked to a combination of company, business unit and team performance.

Each month, Scottish Water's performance against each key performance area is published to all employees. Called "Performance at a Glance", the results are discussed at business unit level. People work through budgets and discuss ways of making the required efficiency savings in their department. Employees can also see how much bonus will be earned on the basis of current performance, so there is an on-going incentive to make sure the targets are met.

Outcomes and Learning Points

Results to date include the following:

- Consistency in HR and reward practices across the company. This is reflected in the results of Scottish Water's climate survey which is run every six months
- Absenteeism rate has reduced from 7.5% to 3%
- Total cost of contracted and casual overtime fell by 18.2% from 2003/04 to 2004/05, and fell by a further 10.5% from 2004/05 to 2005/06.

Andrew Walker again:

"The partnership approach has been absolutely crucial in transforming Scottish Water from a start-up business to a sustainable company. We wouldn't have achieved that without partnership. As we move forward, we will face new challenges and we must ensure our reward policy evolves accordingly."

The Together Company – a journey worth making

The Together Company is about people working together – for customers, for shareholders and for their colleagues. But it can't be created overnight: it's a journey which takes time and the commitment of everybody – yes everybody. The journey starts with employees understanding what success depends on and what they can expect to receive in return. At Accor UK & Ireland Hotels employees were involved in developing the company's vision and values. At David Lloyd Leisure, Spirit to Inspire and WINcard form the platform for engaging people in the things that matter most to club members, people and investors. WINcard is linked to reward too. And it's simply because reward is a powerful communicator of values, direction and business priorities, that it plays such a key part in the journey to become and remain a Together Company.

Together Companies mix and match financial and non-financial rewards in ways that are right for the organisation and its employees, rather than solely on the basis of what the competition is doing. They achieve this through the three-part reward framework:

- Reward Essentials
- Reward Choices
- Reward Extras.

Reward Essentials are the foundation of all reward practices in The Together Company. Getting them right and excelling at them builds employees trust and is far more important than rushing to introduce fancy reward schemes which somebody, somewhere, "thinks" are a good idea. This approach has served Scottish Water extremely well, as it faced tough efficiency targets and a suspicious workforce during its journey from a fledgling company to a sustainable business.

People's behaviour is important to business success in The Together Company, which is why BAA and Scottish Water include it in their performance management and review process. Honest conservations are at the centre of the Performance Review Process at David Lloyd Leisure. The pay framework at Manchester United is firmly rooted to the company's vision and values.

From the vast array of reward practices at its disposal, The Together Company makes a few key Reward Choices which support its business priorities. Rewarding performance features strongly in all of them. ABB Engineering Services (ABB ES) rewards individuals for outstanding customer service and teamwork – as seen by customers. At Miller Insurance Services (Miller) employees are rewarded for performance through base salary and incentives that are linked to individual performance objectives / targets and the financial success of Miller.

Teamwork is a vital ingredient of "togetherness" and we see this reflected in team incentives (financial and non-financial) at The Royal Bank of Scotland Group (RBS), Starbucks and ABB ES. At RBS, team incentives are linked to sales and customer service excellence, while Starbucks rewards achievements that reflect one or more of the six guiding principles of its Mission Statement.

The Together Company also rewards people for the financial success which they help create – group profit sharing and share ownership at RBS and share acquisition at ABB ES, for example. In some companies, BAA for example, senior managers are encouraged to reinvest bonus payments in the business and maintain a significant personal shareholding.

Finally, The Together Company knows that, if it's to stand head and shoulders above the competition, it has to go to beyond Reward Essentials and Reward Choices – which is where Reward Extras come in. These include customising reward packages to reflect people's lifestyles and stages through, for example flexible benefits and flexible working arrangements. RBS and many other leading companies do this.

Recognition and celebration in Together Companies communicate what's important – at T.G.I. Friday's it's part of the culture, whether it's given for improving skills or "wowing" guests with outstanding customer service. Simply letting people know which rewards they're eligible for, how much they're worth to employees and keeping them up-to-date about reward practices is a "must-do" for Together Companies. RBS is a leader in reward communications.

But these things aren't sufficient to attract and retain talented people. Talented people look for a rewarding workplace which provides intangible "soft" rewards, such as job interest, challenge, social interaction and opportunities to develop. A pleasant working environment – as we saw at Microsoft – is part of the equation too.

My challenge to you

I believe becoming a Together Company is within the reach of any organisation. And as you will have realised by now, there's no panacea for becoming one. But the prize is too great to ignore: a company that is a leader in everything it does; a company that attracts and retains the best people; a company whose reward practices reflect the needs of the business and the needs of its people.

I hope that this book has given you practical ideas about reward that you can implement back in the workplace. I hope this book has inspired you to become a Together Company – rewarding what matters most to people and organisations. Will you take up the challenge?

References

Chapter 1

[1] www.johnlewispartnership.co.uk (2006)

[2] Ristretto (Starbucks bi-monthly magazine) (May/June 2005)

[3] Collins, James C. & Porras, Jerry I. (1997) Built to Last, Successful Habits of Visionary Companies, Random House Business Books

[4] Schultz, Howard. (1997) Pour Your Heart Into It, Hyperion, New York

[5] IDS HR Studies Update 769, March 2004

[6] Kaplan, Robert S., and Norton, David P., (1996) The Balanced Scorecard, Harvard Business School Press, Boston

[7] Heskett, James L., Sasser Jr., W. Earl and Schlesinger, Leonard A., (2003) The Value-Profit Chain, The Free Press, New York

[8] Whitbread PLC Annual Review and Summary Report 2005/6

Chapter 2

[1] Zingheim, Patricia, K., & Schuster, Jay R., (2000) Pay People Right, Jossey-Bass, San Fransisco

[2] Brown, Duncan & Armstrong, Michael, (1999) Paying for Contribution, Kogan Page, London

[3] Gratton, Lynda (2000) Living Strategy, Financial Times Prentice Hall, Harlow

Chapter 3

[1] Jane Weightman, (1994) Competencies in Action, Chartered Institute of Personnel and Development, London

[2] Adapted from Whiddett, S and Hollyforde, S., (1999) The Competencies Handbook, Chartered Institute of Personnel and Development, London

Chapter 4

[1] Armstrong, Michael, (1994) Performance Management, Kogan Page, London

[2] Lawler, Edward, E., (2000) Rewarding Excellence, Jossey-Bass, San Fransisco

Chapter 5

[1] Adapted from Armstrong, Michael and Murlis, Helen, (1994) A Handbook of Remuneration Strategy and Practice, Kogan Page, London

[2] Adapted from Armstrong, Michael and Baron, Angela, (1996) The Job Evaluation Handbook, Chartered Institute of Personnel and Development, London

Chapter 6

[1] Chartered Institute of Personnel and Development, (June 2006) Work-life balance

Fact Sheet, London
[2] www.dti.gov.uk (2006)
[3] Employee Benefits, September 2006, Centaur Media, London

Chapter 7
[1] Equal Opportunities Commission, Code of Practice on Equal Pay

Chapter 8
[1] Lawler, Edward, E III, (2000) Rewarding Excellence, Jossey-Bass, San Francisco
[2] Compensation and Benefits Review, September-October 1995
[3] Robert J. Greene, (Summer 1994) Effective Compensation Strategies for Project-Focused Personnel, ACA Journal

Chapter 9
[1] Heskett, James, L, (1987) Lessons in the Service Sector, Harvard Business Review, Boston
[2] First Direct, Harvard Business School Case Study (1996), Boston

Chapter 10
[1] People Management, (23 February 2006) Chartered Institute of Personnel and Development
[2] www.hp.com (2006)
[3] www.johnlewispartnership.co.uk (2006)
[4] Chartered Institute of Personnel and Development, (July 2005) Employee ownership Fact Sheet, London
[5] IDS HR Study 781, (September 2004) Share incentive plans, Incomes Data Services, London
[6] news.independent.co.uk – (21 February 2006)

Chapter 11
[1] Although Airport Development and Investment Limited, a consortium led by Grupo Ferrovial, took control of BAA on 26 June 2006, this case study has been included in the book because it is an outstanding example of a Together Company
[2] Mintzberg, Henry (November 2004) Enough Leadership, Harvard Business Review
[3] Chamberlain, Colin. (2003) Tolley's Practical Guide to Employee Share Schemes, LexisNexis UK, London
[4] IDS ERC Research File 65, Boardroom incentive report 2004, Incomes Data Services, London
[5] HM Revenue & Customs: (2005) Phantom Share Plans, London
[6] Chamberlain, Colin. (2003) Tolley's Practical Guide to Employee Share Schemes, LexisNexis UK, London
[7] Combined Code on Corporate Governance (2003)

Chapter 12

[1] Employee benefits/Towers Perrin flexible benefits research (2006)
[2] Employee benefits/Halifax voluntary benefits research (2005)
[3] Flexible working: (February 2005) impact and implementation, an employer survey, Chartered Institute of Personnel and Development, London
[4] Employee Benefits Awards (2006)

Chapter 13

[1] Zingheim, Patricia, K. and Schuster, Jay, R., (2000) Pay People Right, Jossey-Bass, San Francisco

Chapter 14

[1] Robinson, D, Perryman, S and Hayday, S, (2004) The Drivers of Employee Engagement, Institute for Employment Studies, Brighton
[2] Bevan, S., Barber, L and Robinson, D.,(1997) Keeping the Best: a practical guide to retaining key employees, Institute for Employment Studies, Brighton
[3] Maister, David H. (2001) Practice What You Preach, The Free Press, New York
[4] Maister, David H. (2001) Practice What You Preach, The Free Press, New York
[5] O'Malley, Michael N., (2000) Creating Commitment, John Wiley & Sons, New York
[6] Buckingham, Marcus & Coffman, Curt, (2001) First, Break All the Rules, Simon & Schuster, London
[7] Sunday Times 100 Best Small Companies to Work For (2006)
[8] Sunday Times 100 Best Companies to Work For (2006)
[9] www.microsoft.com/uk (2006)
[10] Bell, Adryan, (2000) Transforming your workplace, Chartered Institute of Personnel and Development, London
[11] Sunday Times 100 Best Small Companies to Work For (2006)

Chapter 15

[1] Wilson, Thomas B., (1999) Rewards that Drive High Performance, American Management Association, New York

Chapter 16

[1] Cadbury Schweppes Press Release, (1 December 2004)
[2] Cadbury Schweppes Press Release, (11 July 2005)
[3] www: cadburyschweppes.com, (March 2006)
[4] Heskett, James L., Sasser Jr., W. Earl and Schlesinger, Leonard A., (2003) The Value-Profit Chain, The Free Press, New York
[5] www.tescocorporate.com (2006)
[6] Tesco Corporate Responsibility Review (2005)
[7] news.independent.co.uk – 21 February (2006)

[8] The Royal Bank of Scotland Group, Annual Review and Summary Financial Statement (2005)

[9] Sunday Times 100 Best Companies to Work For (2006)

[10] The Royal Bank of Scotland Group, Annual Review and Summary Financial Statement (2005)

[11] IDS HR Studies Update 769, March 2004, Incomes Data Services, London

[12] People Management, (23 February 2006)

[13] www.johnlewispartnership.co.uk (2006)

[14] Verdict Consumer Satisfaction Index Top 10, (2006)

[15] www.johnlewispartnership.co.uk (2006)

[16] Sunday Times 100 Best Companies to Work For (2006)

[17] www: dlapiper.com (2006)

[18] www.astrazeneca.co.uk (2006)

[19] AstraZeneca PLC Forth Quarter and Full Results (2005)

Index

Notes

Notes

Notes